A Kid's Guide TO Southern California

GULLIVER TRAVELS

A Kid's Guide TO Southern California

Gulliver Books

Harcourt Brace Jovanovich, Publishers

San Diego   New York   London

C·O·N·T·E·N·T·S

How to Use This Book   **1**

Where Are We Going?   **5**

WHAT'S IT LIKE THERE?   5

GETTING THERE   8

GETTING AROUND   10

LET'S GET STARTED   12

When Did They Do That?   **14**

NATIVE AMERICANS   14

UNDER SPANISH AND MEXICAN RULE   15

STATEHOOD AND BEYOND   21

LIGHTS, CAMERA, ACTION!   22

Can I Have That?   **24**

SHOPPING   24

SOUVENIRS AND GIFTS   25

When Will We Eat?   **29**

LOS ANGELES   **35**

Are There Any Animals?   **38**

THE L.A. ZOO   38

What's That?   **40**

DOWNTOWN L.A.   40

EL PUEBLO DE LOS ANGELES   42

LITTLE TOKYO   42

CHINATOWN   43

L.A. CHILDREN'S MUSEUM   43

LA BREA TAR PITS   44

L.A. COUNTY MUSEUM OF ART   45

EXPOSITION PARK   47

GRIFFITH PARK   51

HOLLYWOOD   53

WESTWOOD   56

SANTA MONICA BEACH   56

SPRUCE GOOSE AND *QUEEN MARY*   58

Will We Have Any Fun?   **59**

    DISNEYLAND   59

    KNOTT'S BERRY FARM   63

    MAGIC MOUNTAIN   66

    RAGING WATERS   68

    NBC STUDIO TOUR   70

    UNIVERSAL STUDIOS TOUR   71

Outside Los Angeles   **73**

    CATALINA ISLAND   73

    ANZA BORREGO DESERT STATE PARK   73

    PALM SPRINGS   74

    IDYLLWILD   75

    DEATH VALLEY   75

SAN DIEGO   **76**

Are There Any Animals?   **79**

    THE SAN DIEGO ZOO   79

    SAN DIEGO WILD ANIMAL PARK   82

    SEA WORLD   84

    SCRIPPS AQUARIUM   89

What's That?   **90**

    BALBOA PARK   90

    SAN DIEGO BAY   98

    NAUTICAL MUSEUMS   98

    CORONADO ISLAND   101

    SHELTER ISLAND   102

    CABRILLO POINT   103

    OLD TOWN   104

    MISSION BAY PARK   105

    PACIFIC BEACH AND MISSION BEACH   106

    LA JOLLA COVE   107

    CHILDREN'S MUSEUM OF SAN DIEGO   108

Outside San Diego   **109**

    TORREY PINES STATE RESERVE   109

    CUYAMACA STATE PARK   110

    JULIAN   112

South of the Border   **113**

Is That All?   **114**

Calendar of Events   **116**

Appendix   **119**

Car Games   **123**

Answers to Puzzles   **127**

Photo Credits   **132**

Index   **133**

How to Use This Book

Are you about to visit Southern California? Read this book before you leave, then carry it with you while you're there. It will help you choose where you want to go each day.

But don't just read it! Write in this book. Color some of the pictures. Keep track of your trip in the travel diary. Use the maps: Try to figure out where you are and where you want to go. There are games and puzzles all through the book for you to do while riding in a car or plane, waiting to eat, or just hanging around waiting for the grown-ups to get going!

The first part of the book tells you what the weather is like in Southern California—you'll want to bring a swimsuit and you won't need your winter coat!

T·R·A·V·E·L D·I·A·R·Y

My name is _____

I live at _____

in _____

My phone number is (_____) _____ — _____

I'm taking a trip through Southern California from _____

_____ to _____. I'm traveling with

_____, and we plan to be away for _____ days.

My parents' full names are _____

and _____. In case of

emergency, they can be reached at _____

or you can call _____

at (_____) _____ — _____.

❖ ❖ ❖

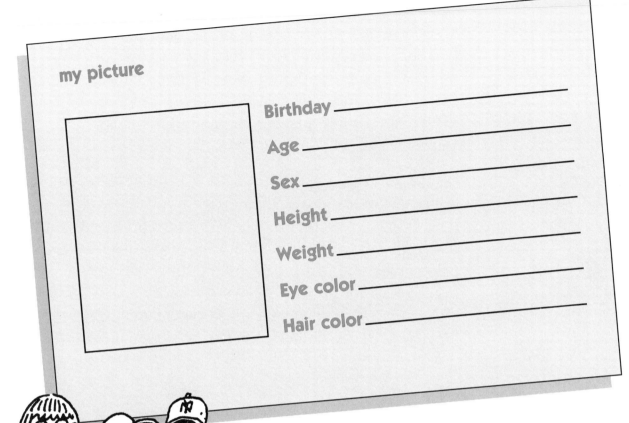

my picture

Birthday _____

Age _____

Sex _____

Height _____

Weight _____

Eye color _____

Hair color _____

Following this introduction are three chapters about the history, shopping, and food of Southern California. Then there is a section about Los Angeles (or L.A., which is how many people refer to the city) and a section about San Diego.

The calendar of events will let you know what special annual activities are going on while you're in Southern California.

For particular information about a place you want to visit, like the time it opens, the address, or the phone number, look in the appendix. Following the appendix, you'll find a number of games you can play in the car, the answers to the puzzles in this book, and the index.

3

You don't have to write only in the blanks in this book. Color and draw wherever there's room, or on top of the pictures already here. Wherever there's room, write about the places you have seen. And there are no right answers to put in the blanks. You can make up whatever you want!

It's fun to keep a journal of your trip. In addition to filling in the travel diary, you may want to use a notebook to write down details of interesting or funny things that happened on your trip. Also, save your ticket stubs and brochures to tape into your journal. Leave room for photographs and your own illustrations. It's your journal, so be creative. It's a great way to remember your trip when it's over.

Today we flew in a hot air balloon! It was terrific. It was so quiet and beautiful. Everything below looked like a toy town.

SKY RIDES
70 48180
D

My ticket from the balloon ride.

Where Are We Going?

WHAT'S IT LIKE THERE?

The sun shines and the temperature's mild most of the time in Southern California, so you'll be able to do lots of things outdoors all year round. The climate is known as Mediterranean because it is much like the climate around the Mediterranean Sea, which is between southern Europe, the Middle East, and northern Africa. Along the coast of Southern California it's rarely above 85 degrees in summer and rarely below 40 degrees in winter. Rain usually falls only in the winter.

The Pacific Ocean helps to make the summers cool and the winters warm in Southern California. Hot Santa Ana winds blow in from the desert and the temperature can climb into the 80's even in the winter, but the humidity falls way down, so everyone stays cool.

Wide, sandy beaches that are easy to get to and fun to play on cover much of the Southern California coast. Some of the shoreline is edged with bluffs and cliffs

Did you know?

It has snowed only twice in San Diego since 1871. Snow fell in 1949, but melted before it hit the ground. It snowed again in 1967, but stayed just long enough to be measured!

5

Trace your route to Southern California

Whether by car, train, bus, or airplane, there was a route you had to follow to reach your destination. Color in the state where you live and draw a line tracing your path from home to vacation spot.

that are great for exploring. Just north of San Diego, near downtown La Jolla, you can go inside a cave that the sea has formed. Along the shoreline of the Palos Verdes Hills, just south of Los Angeles, there are marine terraces that look like giant stone staircases. The lines on these terraces show the different sea levels over the years.

From the taller buildings in downtown L.A., you can—on a clear day—look out over the ocean and see the islands of Santa Catalina and San Nicholas, which are really the peaks of submerged mountain ranges. If you look inland you'll see the peaks of more mountain ranges.

Did you know?

The San Andreas Fault is 650 miles long and ranges from 100 yards to 1 mile wide.

■ ■ ■

There are hundreds of little faults running through the ground in California. It is not uncommon to feel the ground trembling a few times a year with very minor earthquakes.

From the tip of Point Loma in San Diego, looking inland over the city, you can see mountains ranging south into Mexico. If you look toward the ocean you can see the Coronado Islands seventeen miles to the south, off the Mexican coast. The movement of the earth deep under the ground is pushing these mountains upward—which is why we say they're still growing! This is the same underground movement that causes California's occasional earthquakes and landslides.

The surface of the earth is divided into huge plates or segments that are continually shifting. The San Andreas Fault, which runs about two-thirds the length of California, is a big crack between two of these huge, shifting plates. The crack means that the earth has done a lot of moving around here.

7

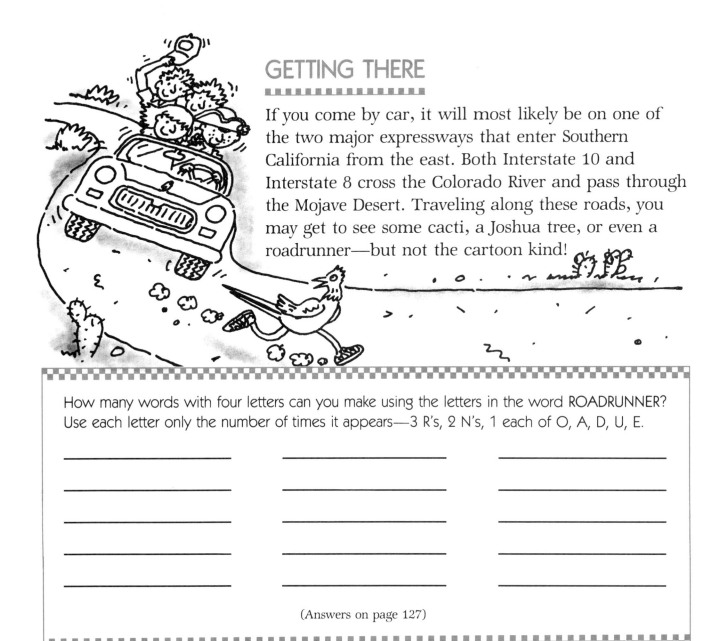

GETTING THERE

If you come by car, it will most likely be on one of the two major expressways that enter Southern California from the east. Both Interstate 10 and Interstate 8 cross the Colorado River and pass through the Mojave Desert. Traveling along these roads, you may get to see some cacti, a Joshua tree, or even a roadrunner—but not the cartoon kind!

How many words with four letters can you make using the letters in the word ROADRUNNER? Use each letter only the number of times it appears—3 R's, 2 N's, 1 each of O, A, D, U, E.

_____   _____   _____

_____   _____   _____

_____   _____   _____

_____   _____   _____

_____   _____   _____

(Answers on page 127)

Interstate 5 runs the length of the West Coast, from the Canadian border to the Mexican border. About 800 miles of it lie in California. Traveling on this freeway between Los Angeles and San Diego, you'll see one city after another, except during a short stretch at Camp Pendleton Marine base and San

Onofre nuclear power plant. You'll have to get off Interstate 5 to get to the beaches, but while on the freeway, you will have a spectacular view of the Pacific Ocean.

Many people come to Southern California by plane. Los Angeles International Airport—LAX for short—handles over 370,000 planes a year. San Diego's Lindbergh Field is named for Charles Lindbergh, the first person to fly alone across the Atlantic Ocean. Both airports are near the Pacific Ocean, so as you land you'll get great views of the hills and canyons reaching right down to the water's edge. If you arrive at night, look for the line where the sparkle of the city lights ends and the pure black of the open sea begins.

Did you know?

Lindbergh's plane, the *Spirit of St. Louis*, was built in San Diego. A replica is housed in the Aerospace Museum in Balboa Park.

International airports use pictures as symbols to let people know what's there. This is because people speak different languages. The symbols let travelers, no matter what their language, find their way around.
Can you match these symbols with their names?

post office
bathroom
train service
helicopter
restaurant
for the disabled
car rental
nursery
telephones
first aid

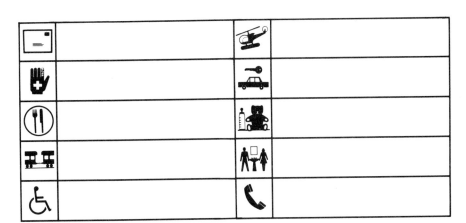

(Answers on page 127)

GETTING AROUND
▪▪▪▪▪▪▪▪▪▪▪▪▪▪▪▪▪▪▪▪

Almost everyone in California travels by car. To go more than a few miles in any direction means you'll most likely travel by freeway. Californians probably believe that they *invented* the freeway—not true, but California does have more miles of freeway than any other state.

The truck wants to go east. Both the car and the van want to go west. Can you help them get where they want to go by making only right turns?

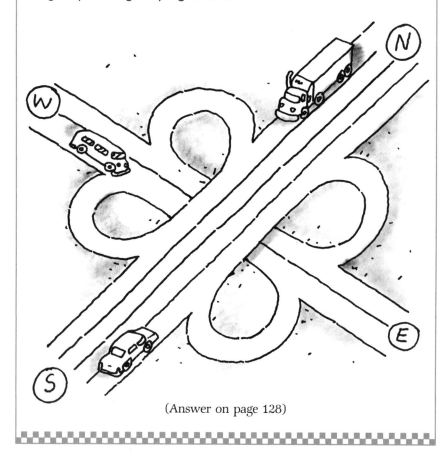

(Answer on page 128)

Did you know?

There are over 6,500 miles of roads and freeways inside the Los Angeles city limits alone.

If you've never been on a train, here's your chance. Southern California offers not one, but two kinds of trains. If you want to ride on a real train—one with a full-size engine, conductors, engineers, and a dining car—then climb aboard Amtrak. Amtrak trains make eight trips a day up and down the coast between Los Angeles and San Diego.

The San Diego trolleys are electric trains that get their power from overhanging wires that look like telephone lines. For about the cost of a bus ride, you can take a trolley to Mexico and walk across the border. If you get to the station just as a trolley is pulling away, don't worry—there'll be another one in 15 minutes. All aboard!

Did you know?

The trolleys travel through San Diego at up to 50 miles per hour. They can take you from the heart of San Diego to the Mexican border in just 40 minutes.

LET'S GET STARTED

Since weather is never—or hardly ever—a problem, most days you can swim, surf, snorkel, sail on the ocean, or just take a cruise around one of the bays.

T·R·A·V·E·L D·I·A·R·Y

We will be leaving _____ on _____

and arriving in _____ on _____.

We will travel by _____, and it

should take us about _____.

We have to travel through _____ to get

to Southern California. Once we get there, we will stay at

_____

_____

We plan to visit all these places on our trip: _____

_____.

I am _____ hours/ _____ days/ _____ miles away

from home.

❖ ❖ ❖

There are great zoos in Los Angeles and San Diego, and special parks where you can see animals in their natural habitats. You'll be able to get really close to some fascinating sea creatures, like dolphins, otters, penguins, and even killer whales. Well, *you* can get as close as you like to the whales!

What if you get lost?

Make sure you agree with your parents about what to do if you should get lost. Should you stay where you are, or look for the nearest lost and found, the nearest police officer, the information center, the closest tree? Talk about it before each adventure.

Southern California is packed with museums and wonderful amusement parks that have been designed especially for kids. Take a look at the luxury ocean liner *Queen Mary* and the *Spruce Goose*, the largest airplane ever built—they're waiting for you in Long Beach. And if you get dizzy from all the activity, you can always take a walk or have a run on the beach, build a giant sandcastle, or just wiggle your toes in the sand and watch the sun drop down over the water at the end of the day.

When Did They Do That?

NATIVE AMERICANS

Scientists still argue about how long people have been living on the beautiful beaches of Southern California, but it's been at least 20,000 years! When the Spanish discovered this part of the world about 450 years ago, thousands of American Indians lived in small villages on some of the same beaches, canyons, mountains, and deserts you will visit while you're here.

You can get an idea of what Southern California looked like back then if you visit Balboa Park in San Diego. Some of the native oak trees have been preserved in the canyons around the outside of the park. The early Indians ate the nuts, seeds, berries, and fruits that grow wild here. They also ate fish. In small boats made of bundled reeds, they paddled way out into the ocean to go deep-sea fishing. They collected and traded seashells with other tribes to buy

Did you know?

Acorns were the American Indians' main staple. They ground them up, boiled out the bitterness, and cooked them like hot cereal.

things they could not get or make themselves. The shells from these beaches have been found as far away as the Great Plains—other Indian tribes across the country passed them along in their trading. You can learn about these American Indians at the Museum of Man in Balboa Park.

Did you know?

California has a larger population of American Indians than any other state in the country—about 198,000.

Did you know?

Pictographs—pictures painted or carved in rocks by the Indians—can be found in the mountains and deserts of Southern California.

■ ■ ■

The name *California* came from a fifteenth-century Spanish novel. It was the name of an imaginary island of Amazons ruled by Queen Calafia.

■ ■ ■

More people move to California each day than came during the first 100 years after Cabrillo discovered it.

UNDER SPANISH AND MEXICAN RULE

In the mid-1500s Spanish explorers traveled the coast of Mexico conquering people and claiming land for their king. Two of their ships, under the command of Juan Cabrillo, were sent north to explore the coast. In September of 1542, Cabrillo became the first European to sail into what we now know as San Diego Harbor. He and his men were enchanted by the beauty of the land and the friendliness of the Indians, and they claimed California for Spain as a Mexican state—without a single battle. Today, the land is still beautiful and the people just as friendly! On the tip of Point Loma in San Diego, you can visit Cabrillo National Monument to get a spectacular view of the harbor and the impressive U.S. naval base across the bay on Coronado Island. Right near the monument, the lighthouse that served the harbor between 1855 and 1891 has been restored.

About 200 years after Cabrillo claimed California for Spain, a small group of Franciscan missionaries led by Father Junipero Serra left Baja California and came north to convert the Indians of California to Christianity and win their allegiance to Spain. They

Did you know?

Baja California is the 760-mile-long peninsula in Mexico, just south of San Diego. *Baja* means "lower" in Spanish. When California was part of Mexico, it was called Alta California—which means "upper California."

Did you know?

The Franciscans established 21 missions in California, from San Diego in Southern California, to Sonoma in northern California.

■ ■ ■

If the swallows aren't at the mission, you can still feed the many white doves that live there all year round.

established their first mission in 1769—San Diego de Alcala. You can see a restoration of the mission building about 15 minutes from downtown San Diego, off Mission Gorge Road. Mission de San Juan Capistrano, located north of San Diego, is probably the most well known California mission. The famous swallows return here from their winter nesting grounds in Argentina, South America, around St. Joseph's Day (March 19). You may not see any swallows during your visit, but you can see their nests all around the mission, which is the oldest building in California.

SPEAK AND SPELL

How would you pronounce Cabrillo? Remember, you'd pronounce Baja as BAH-hah. How would you pronounce . . .

Alcala?
Capistrano?
San Juan?
Junipero Serra?

(Answers on page 128)

Forts were built to protect the missions, and towns called *presidios* grew up around them. San Diego was once a presidio, but all that's left now of the presidio is a park. Just below Presidio Park is Old Town, which was the center of San Diego in the 1800s. You can visit many old preserved houses that have been moved here, and lots of new shops and restaurants, too.

Los Angeles was one of California's first independent settlements, or *pueblos.* In 1781, eleven families of Indian, Spanish, black, and mixed heritage settled here together. The settlement was called El Pueblo de Nuestra Señora la Reina de Los Angeles de Porciuncula, meaning "The Pueblo of Our Lady, the Queen of Angels." Today, we just call it Los Angeles

---

Fill in the blanks below to discover my hiding place.

__ __ __ __ __ __ __ __ __   He discovered San Diego Bay.

__ __ __ __ __ __ __ __   San Juan Capistrano is one.

__ __ __ __   __ __ __ __ __   The first mission was built here.

__ __ __ __ __ __ __   First established by land grant in 1775.

__ __ __ __ __ __   Built to protect early missions.

__ __ __ __ __ __   "Knight in Buckskin"

__ __ __ __ __ __ __ __ __   Towns built around forts.

__ __ __ __   Skins sought by trappers.

__ __ __ __ __   Spanish word for "saint."

__ __ __ __ __   Franciscan friar.

(Answers on page 128)

or L.A. The Old Plaza, a 44-acre state historical park located in the center of the city, marks the area of the original pueblo. It has lots of shops, restaurants, and entertainment spots, and many historical buildings that date back to the city's Mexican beginnings.

Did you know?

The cowboys on California ranchos (that's "ranches" to us) were called *vaqueros* (vah-KAY-rohs). One cattle hide was worth about one dollar—and was called a "California banknote."

■ ■ ■

Southern California now gets most of its water from the biggest irrigation system in the world, the giant California aqueduct.

The first California rancho was established in 1775. For many years, cattle hides from the ranchos were sent east to be made into shoes. They were California's most important export.

Aqueducts were built to capture water and transport it to the ranchos. These new sources of water made it possible for everyone, including the Indians and missionaries, to grow food. Just about anything will grow in the hot sun and mild nights of California.

Soon farmers and ranchers throughout Southern California were raising crops and animals to sell. They would gather at large open markets and trade their produce. To this day, there are still county fairs where farmers and ranchers display their products. You can go to one of the nation's largest fairs, the L.A. County Fair in Pomona, where you'll see animals sold in big public show-rings.

During the Gold Rush of 1848, the population of California boomed. People came from all over the country and the world hoping to find gold in the hills of California. Most of it was found in northern California, and a few people *did* strike it rich. But the rest soon had to find other ways to make a living.

WORD SCRAMBLE

The letters in the names below are all mixed up.
Can you unscramble them?

laCirbol _____

friniCaloa _____

osL sleenAg _____

scarFincans _____

ontiP moaL _____

bolaBa kaPr _____

veNait manerAcsi _____

anS egDoi _____

(Answers on page 128)

Many turned to farming to feed all the new Californians. About an hour east of San Diego, you can visit one of the few Southern California gold mining towns, called Julian. It is also known for its apple orchards.

STATEHOOD AND BEYOND

Whaling ships from New England and ships bringing spices from China stopped to take advantage of Southern California's natural harbors and mild weather.

In 1826 a fur trapper from New England named Jedediah Smith blazed a trail overland from the Great Salt Lake in Utah to Los Angeles. He had a battle with a grizzly bear—a battle Jedediah must have won—and became known as the "Knight in Buckskin." His pioneering opened the way for more and more settlers from the East, and in 1850 California became the thirty-first state in the Union.

LIGHTS, CAMERA, ACTION!

Horace Wilcox was a very quiet, peace-loving man who thought that Los Angeles was too sinful. In the late 1880s he turned his ranch, which was near Los Angeles, into its own little town. His wife named the town Hollywood, and they encouraged only quiet, peaceful people like themselves to settle there. They certainly didn't know what was about to happen! Some twenty years later, the mild weather, friendly natives, and beautiful scenery once again lured people to Southern California—this time they came to Hollywood to make movies. Dozens of production companies sprang up, outraging the very proper Hollywood families. The original townsfolk would have liked to throw out the "gypsies," as they called the actors, but the movie people were there to stay.

Did you know?

The first California-made movie was a short one-reeler called *Across the Divide*. It was filmed in 1908 in a rented Chinese laundry.

ENTERTAINMENT TRIVIA

1. Before motion pictures became popular, Los Angeles was known for its _____ .
   a) palm trees   b) orange groves   c) beaches

2. Motion pictures were introduced in the _____ .
   a) 1920s   b) 1930s   c) 1940s

3. "Go West, young man!" was _____ advice to Americans over 130 years ago.
   a) Abraham Lincoln's   b) Horace Greeley's   c) Jedediah Smith's

4. In Los Angeles the entertainment industry—the major economic and social force in the area—is known as _____ .
   a) The Flicks   b) The Business   c) The Industry

5. Today only one major studio, _____ , has its offices in Hollywood proper. The rest have moved to surrounding areas.
   a) Paramount Studios   b) Universal Studios   c) Columbia Pictures

6. Ronald Reagan has been not only president of the United States, he's also been _____ .
   a) president of The Screen Actors Guild   b) governor of California   c) both

7. The annual awards given in the television industry are known as _____ .
   a) The Emmy Awards   b) The Oscars   c) The Golden Globe Awards

8. _____ led a new movement in the 1960s known as surf music.
   a) The Beach Boys   b) Annette Funicello   c) The Mamas and Papas

9. Los Angeles, along with _____ and _____ , is considered one of the homes of the music industry.
   a) Chicago/New York   b) New York/Nashville   c) Chicago/Nashville

(Answers on page 128)

Production companies built bigger and better studios, using their "back lots" to create every imaginable type of setting. These same studios are used today to film TV shows and cartoons. Movies and television shows are produced all over the world, but Los Angeles is still the film capital.

Did you know?

Walt Disney's first cartoon movie—starring Mickey Mouse—was filmed in Hollywood.

Can I Have That?

SHOPPING

No trip is complete without something to show the kids back home. Shopping is a favorite sport of Southern Californians, and you'll come across street vendors, small shops, big stores, or gigantic shopping malls wherever you go. Everything is available, from the very latest and most elegant fashions of Beverly Hills' Rodeo Drive to serapes and piñatas in Tijuana. All the museums and parks, even the zoos, have souvenirs you can buy to remind you of your trip long after you get home.

SPEAK AND SPELL

The "rodeo" of Rodeo Drive is pronounced *roh-DAY-oh*.

In Spanish:

ñ = ny

so piñata is pronounced *peen-YAH-tah*. How would you pronounce serape (a type of woven cape or poncho)? How about Tijuana?

(Answers on page 128)

Did you know?

A piñata is a decorative container usually made of papier-mâché and filled with goodies that Mexican children break open on their birthdays and holiday celebrations.

24

T·R·A·V·E·L D·I·A·R·Y

On our trip, we are staying ___with friends ___with relatives ___in a hotel ___at a campground ___in the zoo. I packed _____ to bring with me on this trip because I know I will need it/them to _____ _____. I forgot to bring along _____, but I brought _____ to play with. I brought _____ dollars to spend on souvenirs. I want to buy _____ at _____

❖ ❖ ❖

SOUVENIRS AND GIFTS

California is a place where people of many different cultures have come together, and downtown Los Angeles is full of areas where you can experience these different cultures. Mexican handicrafts are

25

abundant in the shops of Olvera Street. The "Street of the Golden Palace" in the heart of Chinatown offers wonderful Chinese gifts. And you can find a lot of beautiful things from Japan in the area called Little Tokyo. The sights, smells, and tastes you'll find in these and other neighborhoods make a visit worthwhile—even if you don't buy anything! Los Angeles also has two big outdoor markets—the Farmers Market and the Grand Central Public Market—where there's something for everyone.

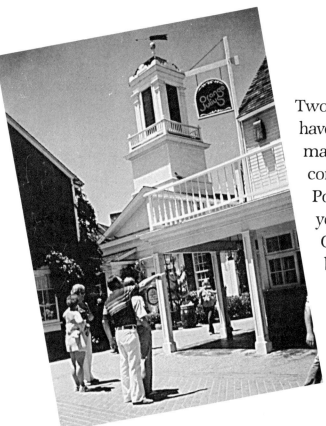

Two shopping "villages" located near the ocean have shops just for kids. **Ports O' Call**, near the main entrance to Los Angeles Harbor, combines a New England fishing port with a Polynesian village—a unique blend you'll probably find only in California! Ports O' Call has over eighty shops, streets brightened by gaslights, and most exciting of all, helicopter rides.

Did you know?

The Broadway Flying Horses is one of 300 carousels created with real hand-carved wooden animals. Its original home was Coney Island, New York, at the turn of the century; it was later moved to Salisbury Beach, Massachusetts. Seaport Village craftsmen spent more than 2 years restoring it.

Spend some time at **Seaport Village**, which faces San Diego Bay. The shops here, too, are fashioned to look like what you'd find in an East Coast fishing village. There's a chocolate-chip cookie store and a shop where you can watch fudge being made in the window. San Diegans, young and old, love to fly kites. You can buy kites in crazy shapes—like a butterfly or a sea serpent—to fly in the Seaport Village park or to take home. Stroll along the pier, ride in a horse-drawn carriage, mount a wooden horse on the Broadway Flying Horses Carousel, or visit the Mukiteo Lighthouse—a copy of a real lighthouse in Everett, Washington. Then go to the teddy bear store, where you can buy any kind or size of bear you want, and clothes to put on it, too.

If you're passing through downtown San Diego, don't miss a visit to **Horton Plaza.** It's a shopping center, and much more. There are paths, bridges, patios, courtyards, and shops on many levels, painted different colors and facing every which way. It's wonderful to wander through and a great place to watch people. But be careful: it's also very easy to get lost.

Here you will find stores full of games, toys, kites, candy, and clothes just for kids. And on your way to one of the seven theaters on the top level, you will pass by all of your favorite foods. The cinnamon roll, french fries, and ice cream shops are especially popular. While you snack you can look down to the main courtyard and watch a show. There are almost always musicians, mimes, or jugglers to entertain you.

When Will We Eat?

Southern California is full of fun places to eat. If you're a sailor at heart, you can eat while sailing in San Diego Bay on a windjammer or cruising on Mission Bay on a riverboat. You landlubbers can stay on shore and munch in restaurants that look like everything from railroad cars to Chinese pagodas. One fast-food stand in Hollywood, the Tail of the Pup, is built to look just like a giant hot dog. And of course there are lots of places to eat outdoors—something you can do any time of the year in Southern California.

Not only are there a lot of different-looking places to eat, but there are also all kinds of different foods—African, British, Chinese, French, German, Greek, Hungarian, East Indian, Italian, Japanese, Korean, Mexican, Persian, Polynesian, Thai, Vietnamese, California health food, and good old American.

Because Mexico is right next door and many Mexican-Americans live in California, Mexican restaurants are everywhere. Quite a few are decorated to look like haciendas. Before your meal arrives, you will probably get a plate of tortilla chips that are similar to potato chips, only they are made from corn and shaped like little triangles. The tortilla chips come with a red dip called *salsa*. Don't put too much on one chip—salsa is sometimes very spicy! Tortilla chips can also be dipped in *guacamole*, a very mild dip made from avocados—it looks like green mashed potatoes. The most popular Mexican dishes are burritos, tacos, and enchiladas. They are all made with tortillas, but each has its own shape and its own kind of filling. Traditionally, they are eaten with a helping of rice and refried beans.

The Japanese restaurants are truly exotic, as are other Oriental and Polynesian restaurants. Some have bridges and streams to cross before you get to your table. A few require that you take off your shoes before entering. The tables themselves are sometimes so low that you have to sit on the floor to eat. Some of these restaurants feature food that is cooked at your table by chefs who juggle their knives and cook at the same time.

Many of the Japanese meals include rice and fish. One special Japanese dish is *sushi*—little round cakes of rice filled with seaweed or raw fish. You can even eat octopus arms!

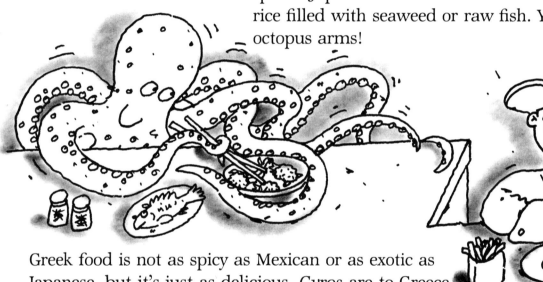

Greek food is not as spicy as Mexican or as exotic as Japanese, but it's just as delicious. *Gyros* are to Greece what hamburgers are to America. Gyros are meat, onions, and tomatoes, covered with a special Greek sauce and wrapped in pita bread. If you really want a treat, ask for *baklava* for dessert. Have your sweet tooth ready. Baklava is nutty, flaky, and very sweet.

Did you know?

Pita bread looks like a thick pizza crust, only smaller around. Sometimes it is wrapped around food; other times it is cut in half and food is stuffed inside—that's why it's also called *pocket bread*.

31

If you want to feast like the kings and queens of the Middle Ages, don't miss a dinner and show at the Medieval Times Castle, near Disneyland and Knott's Berry Farm. When you enter the castle, you are crowned prince or princess and escorted to your table. There you'll be served by waitresses and waiters dressed in medieval costumes. While you eat your four-course feast, you watch knights compete in ancient games and joust on horseback. Merlin the Magician is also there to greet you and delight you with his mystical powers.

California is well known for its fresh and light cuisine. So, for all the people who are health-conscious, there are health-food restaurants. The food is mostly raw or lightly cooked, with lots of fruits, nuts, and vegetables. And of course, there are whole wheat bread, sprouts, and California's "green gold," avocados.

Did you know?

Avocados are a fruit. Most of the avocados eaten in the United States are grown in Southern California. They are picked from trees when they are still as hard as rocks. Only after they've turned soft are they ready to eat.

T·R·A·V·E·L D·I·A·R·Y

While in California, I want to try all these foods:

___taco   ___avocado   ___refried beans

___sushi   ___salsa   ___enchiladas

___burrito   ___wontons   ___juice shake

___baklava   ___guacamole   _____

___gyros   ___tortilla chips   _____

My favorite kind of food is _____.

Of all the food I tasted here in Southern California, I liked _____ the best.

Fun places I ate: What I ate there:

_____   _____

_____   _____

_____   _____

_____

Juice bars are another California favorite. There's one just downstairs from the L.A. Children's Museum. You can have a thick drink like a milkshake made from any kind of fruit you can think of, and wow, are they sweet!

All the different types of restaurants have their own special fun things to see, do, and eat. Be daring. You may be in California, but inside one of these restaurants you can feel like you're just about any place in the world!

There are many kinds of food to eat in Southern California. Match the food with the country it comes from.

burrito	Japan
wonton	England
baklava	Italy
lasagna	China
sushi	Mexico
dumpling	Greece
curry	India

(Answers on page 129)

L·O·S A·N·G·E·L·E·S

What do you think of when you hear the name Los Angeles? Most people think of Hollywood movies and Disneyland, or freeways and friendly, sun-loving people. But what we call Los Angeles is really a bunch of cities, towns, and neighborhoods crammed together and crisscrossed and connected by thousands of miles of roads. It's this nation's second-largest city. Greater Los Angeles—the whole urban area from the mountains to the sea—runs 50 miles from north to south and 30 miles from east to west, and has a population of over 12 million people in 80 cities.

Half of the people living here are originally from some other part of the country or from some other part of the world. People don't just come here for the great weather. L.A. is also the business and trade capital of the western United States. And of course, L.A. is the show-biz capital of the world.

35

T·R·A·V·E·L D·I·A·R·Y

In Los Angeles, we are going to visit all these places: _____

_____

_____

_____

_____

I am most excited about seeing _____

because _____ ,

I have heard all about _____

and I'm going to go there to _____

so I can tell my friends that I _____

❖ ❖ ❖

DO YOU KNOW HOW TO READ A MAP?

Maps are always printed with north up, south down, west left, and east right. (Remember that the sun sets over the Pacific Ocean to the west.) See if you can find the way to where you are going each day.

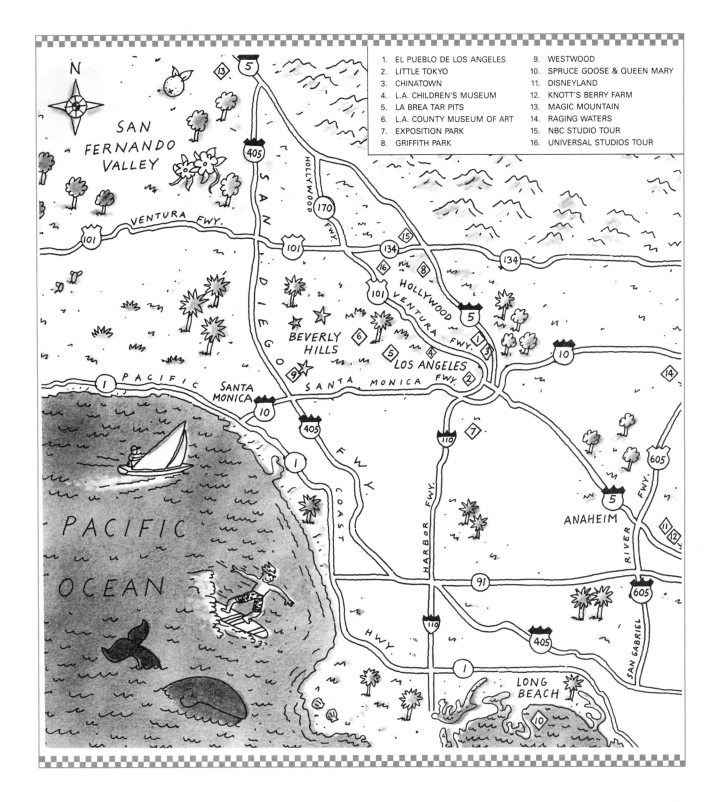

1. EL PUEBLO DE LOS ANGELES
2. LITTLE TOKYO
3. CHINATOWN
4. L.A. CHILDREN'S MUSEUM
5. LA BREA TAR PITS
6. L.A. COUNTY MUSEUM OF ART
7. EXPOSITION PARK
8. GRIFFITH PARK
9. WESTWOOD
10. SPRUCE GOOSE & QUEEN MARY
11. DISNEYLAND
12. KNOTT'S BERRY FARM
13. MAGIC MOUNTAIN
14. RAGING WATERS
15. NBC STUDIO TOUR
16. UNIVERSAL STUDIOS TOUR

Are There Any Animals?

THE L.A. ZOO

You might not expect to find more than 2,000 wild animals in the heart of Los Angeles, but that's exactly what you'll discover at the intersection of the Golden State and Ventura freeways.

Carefully laid out on the eastern edge of Griffith Park, the 113-acre L.A. Zoo is divided into five continental areas. Of special interest are the Australian kangaroos and wallabies, the North American bighorn sheep, the African black rhinoceroses, the Eurasian snow leopards, and the South American jaguars. A Children's Zoo, a Reptile House, and an Aquatics

Center complete the zoo. Special animal shows featuring birds, cats, and elephants are presented daily. And if you're feeling adventurous you can ride an elephant or a camel!

The animals got out of their cages and the zookeeper must find them. Help him locate the animals by circling each word as it is found. Names run up, down, and diagonally—forward and backward.

```
E  P  O  L  E  T  N  A  G  K  L  A  N  J  C
O  T  B  I  O  S  T  R  I  C  H  E  P  A  Z
P  Y  I  R  T  M  O  A  R  H  A  R  M  G  F
A  B  S  G  T  G  I  J  A  V  T  E  O  U  L
C  A  O  Z  E  B  R  A  F  O  L  G  U  A  P
G  L  N  M  R  R  H  E  F  O  P  O  S  R  O
O  L  Q  K  O  A  L  A  E  R  A  S  E  A  L
R  A  B  I  R  N  D  G  E  A  N  O  E  G  A
I  W  J  M  B  R  K  L  X  G  D  V  W  N  R
L  I  O  N  A  F  L  E  D  N  A  F  M  L  B
L  A  N  P  W  G  A  P  Y  A  S  N  A  K  E
A  I  O  V  D  M  D  S  T  K  O  L  J  R  A
S  E  Q  E  A  E  L  U  M  C  O  N  D  O  R
L  H  E  L  E  P  H  A  N  T  K  C  K  U  Y
Z  R  L  P  E  E  H  S  N  R  O  H  G  I  B
```

tiger	polar bear	gorilla	giraffe	antelope
koala	ostrich	lion	camel	deer
condor	snake	zebra	seal	kangaroo
eagle	monkey	elephant	llama	wallaby
otter	owl	panda	mouse	ape
bighorn sheep	jaguar	leopard	bison	mule

(Answers on page 129)

39

What's That?

DOWNTOWN L.A.

It's hard to see the center of the city of Los Angeles, but if you can find where most of the major freeways crisscross, then you've found downtown. Every stage of L.A.'s history can be seen here, from the first pueblo at Olvera Street, to the city's tallest modern skyscraper, the 62-story United California Building.

Downtown is one of the few places in L.A. where it is possible to take a walking tour. Within a few blocks of the grand old City Hall, you can find three important cultural areas—the Hispanic community around the old Pueblo de Los Angeles, the Japanese community in Little Tokyo, and Chinatown. In back of City Hall, you can see one of the last of the great passenger train terminals, Union Station. To the west, the five cylindrical towers of the super-modern Bonaventure Hotel stick straight into the sky. On yet another side, at the edge of Little Tokyo, is the world's only museum of neon art. L.A.'s Visitor's Information Center is also downtown, in the Arco Towers. You can get free maps here and information about things to do in Southern California. And there are guides available who will conduct tours in any one of seven languages.

T·R·A·V·E·L D·I·A·R·Y

People come to Southern California from all over the world, both to live here and to visit. I come from _____.

My parents come from _____.

My ancestors come from _____.

I've seen people from many different countries on this trip.

Some are from:

___China   ___the Philippines   ___France   ___Other

___Japan   ___Australia   ___England   ___

___Mexico   ___India   ___Canada

And I've heard some different languages spoken. Even the English some people speak here sounds different because of their accents. If I ever learn to speak another language, I would choose _____.

because _____

❖ ❖ ❖

EL PUEBLO DE LOS ANGELES

Just a few blocks north of City Hall is the site of El Pueblo de Los Angeles, where the first settlers built their earth-and-willow huts. This is Olvera Street, where you can see inside the oldest standing house in Los Angeles, the Avila Adobe, or walk the stone streets through the Mexican-style market.

The first Catholic church in L.A. is right on the corner of Olvera Street and the Old Plaza. It is still open to the public and has remained a Spanish-speaking church. Just across the square is the Old Plaza Fire Station, which has a big collection of fire helmets on the wall—some of them are 100 years old.

In the Historical Society office, just off the Plaza, you can get a map and see a short film about the pueblo's many historic sites.

Did you know?

The magnolia tree in the center of the Old Plaza is over 100 years old.

■ ■ ■

On weekends you can watch traditional folk dancers and listen to mariachi bands under the shade of the magnolia tree.

LITTLE TOKYO

While you are still downtown, you can walk or take a minibus south about half a mile to Little Tokyo—a century-old Japanese neighborhood. You will know you are there when you see the turned-up roof corners of the Japanese buildings. Everywhere you look there are Japanese restaurants and stores. As in Japan, the restaurants have in their windows plastic food that looks just like the real food you can order inside. See the signs? They all have Japanese writing on them. Each figure stands for a whole word or idea.

CHINESE	JAPANESE	ENGLISH
筷子	箸	chopsticks
雪糕	アイスクリーム	ice cream
西瓜	すいか	watermelon
是	はい	yes

Can you write ice cream in Chinese? _____

Japanese? _____

CHINATOWN

The minibus will also take you half a mile north from Olvera Street to another neighborhood with figures on all the signs. This is Chinatown, and these figures are Chinese. Can you see a difference? Chinese writing is more square than Japanese. The food and toys are all different, too. This is a great place to buy a colorful kite and fortune cookies!

L.A. CHILDREN'S MUSEUM

Downtown is also the home of a museum designed just for kids—the Los Angeles Children's Museum. Here you can touch everything. You can climb into the driver's seat of a city bus or sit in a TV studio and make up the news. You can sing your favorite song in a recording studio and then listen to what you sound like. How about being a clown on the news? You can

Did you know?

The store in the Children's Museum has one of the best selections of kids' books that you'll ever see.

43

paint your face with any colors and shapes you want. For you actors and dancers, there's a dance room with a stage where you can put on a show.

LA BREA TAR PITS

If you go west from downtown toward the beach, stop halfway at Hancock Park. Here, right in the middle of this big city, is the world's richest Ice Age fossil deposit. Scientists have dug over 100 tons of fossils from the famous La Brea Tar Pits. Animals that lived from about 9,000 to 40,000 years ago were trapped in the sticky pools of oil that seep up from deep under the ground. Inside the Page Museum you can see some of the different animals and plants that were preserved by the tar. Remember, these aren't dinosaurs. Dinosaurs were gone 65 million years before these animals lived. Now most of the kinds of animals found in the pits are extinct, too. Can you believe it? Elephants and tigers bigger than any alive in Africa once lived right here.

Did you know?

The gas that bubbles up from the La Brea Tar Pits is the same kind of gas used to heat your house and to cook.

Did you know?

Human fossils have been found in the tar pits, too.

L.A. COUNTY MUSEUM OF ART

The huge concrete building on the west side of Hancock Park is the biggest art museum on the west coast of the United States. The L.A. County Museum of Art has a little bit of everything: costumes, sculptures, weapons, furniture, glass, paintings, pottery, jewelry, baskets, and drawings. Exhibits change frequently so there's always something new to see.

45

T·R·A·V·E·L D·I·A·R·Y

I like _____ art. The best art I have

seen is _____. I like it because

_____. If I made some art for a

museum, it would be _____.

(draw your masterpiece here)

I would like to be an ___artist ___astronaut ___athlete

_____.

because _____

❖ ❖ ❖

EXPOSITION PARK

Five minutes south of downtown is Exposition Park. This is where the 1932 and 1984 Olympic Games were held. On the lawn next to the gigantic sports Coliseum there are signs with the names of all the Olympic cities and the years in which they hosted the games. And, sports fans, on the other side of the park is the University of Southern California—home of the great college baseball and football teams.

The museums in this park are as different inside as they are outside. But don't let the names fool you. They all have things for you to play with inside.

Watch a movie in the eight-sided **Mitsubishi Imax Theater**. The movies are shown on a screen that's seventy feet wide and five stories high in surround-sound that makes you feel like you're part of the action. You may want to skip this if you get motion sickness, because you'll feel like you're moving with the picture. Many different movies are shown throughout the day. Some have actual plots and story lines, some are about science and space, and others

Did you know?

There are 22 official summer Olympic sports.

■ ■ ■

Do you know in which Olympic events women and men compete together?
(Answer on page 129)

T·R·A·V·E·L D·I·A·R·Y

My favorite sport in the Olympics is _____

because _____

I'm best at playing _____

If I were in the Olympics, I would compete in _____

_____

❖ ❖ ❖

Did you know?

The first American woman astronaut, Sally Ride, was born in Los Angeles. She first went into space in 1983.

■ ■ ■

Your heart is a hollow muscle that is about the same size as your fist. It beats about 70 times a minute and about 100,000 times every day.

are cultural, but they are *all* entertaining. In **Aerospace Building Two** and in the **Air and Space Garden,** right behind the theater, there are full-size airplanes and space capsules to walk in and around. Inside **Aerospace Museum One** (it looks like a big gray metal moon station), you can practice flying a spacecraft. Like the inside of a space command center, there are TV screens and computer panels with lots of beeping sounds and flashing green lights. Here you can watch videos of real rockets blasting off, or practice steering your own spaceship.

Next door, in the **California Museum of Science and Industry,** you can take a health test. You get your own plastic card—just like a credit card—to put into each station to take a test. The test examines your eating habits, and your lungs, heart, eyes, ears, balance, and more. When you're all done, a computer prints out your results.

Two other favorite things for kids are downstairs in the farming room. Here you can watch real baby chicks breaking out of their eggs and bees making honey. There are no lazy bees in the colony. Each insect has a job. The bees going through the glass tubes into the wall are on their way outside to the park's rose garden to get pollen for making honey. When they have a full load, they find their way back to their queen. She's the big bee with a red dot painted on her so you can see her better.

HONEY For Sale

Did you know?

Honeybees are the only insects that make food that humans eat. Bees sting only when they are scared or hurt. The queen bee does nothing else but lay eggs all her life.

T·R·A·V·E·L D·I·A·R·Y

I stay healthy because I eat _____.

and get exercise by _____

I also sleep about _____ hours every night, which keeps

my body rested.

❖ ❖ ❖

SPELLING BEE

Can you unscramble these letters and decode the names of these things?

MMSUUE _____

EOBAD _____

SOIFLS _____

STOCKER _____

RAINSOUDS _____

SUNBIIM _____

SLUSPACE _____

TREMPOCU _____

(Answers on page 129)

Three hundred million years of history are waiting for you in the **Los Angeles Museum of Natural History.** It's the big red brick building at the far end of the rose garden. Inside you will find full-size dinosaur skeletons and replicas of animals from every continent on earth. There are African elephants, tigers, wolves, and every kind of lizard and bird you can imagine.

Don't miss the gem and mineral rooms. The rocks you will see are some of nature's most amazing creations—all different colors and strange shapes.

Did you know?

Camels first lived in North America thousands of years ago and then migrated to other parts of the world.

If you like the history of people as much as the history of animals, walk through the American history rooms. Here you can see what life was like for the early pioneers. There are examples of their clothes, furniture, guns, and tools. This stuff might look old to you, but it's all less than 300 years old. But the Egyptian mummy by the front door is over 2,000 years old!

The new triangular building in the corner of the park next to the space theater is the **Afro-American Museum.** In this building there are pictures, papers, books, and art of black Americans who were pioneers, soldiers, scientists, politicians, artists, farmers, and slaves.

Behind all the museums is the Swimming Stadium, where Olympic swimmers raced in the summer of 1984. Now you can swim here in the summertime.

GRIFFITH PARK

For the best view of Los Angeles and the stars, wind your way up to the top of Griffith Park to the observatory and planetarium. Look back over your right shoulder when you're there and you will see the big white Hollywood sign on the hillside. On a clear day, you can see downtown L.A., Hollywood, and all

the way out to Santa Monica Beach. (It does get clear sometimes on windy days.)

On a clear night, you can look through the giant telescope at the moon and the planets Venus and Mars. Day or night you can see stars inside the planetarium, a dome theater. Movies shown here take you on a trip across the sky and through history. Inside the museum are different kinds of telescopes, and pictures of the earth and the moon taken from spaceships and satellites.

The park not only has an observatory, but it also has a zoo, miles of hiking and bridle paths, a model car and miniature train park, and a place to ride ponies.

STARGAZERS

On a clear night, have you ever looked at the stars and seen people or animals? If you have, then you're a stargazer. The stars are out above. Connect the numbered dots in order to discover the hidden zodiac sign.

(Answer on page 129)

HOLLYWOOD

West of Griffith Park, toward the ocean, is the world-famous home of show biz—Hollywood. Today the TV and movie business is spread all over Los Angeles, but there are still some key movieland sites to see here. You need to take a two-hour guided bus tour if you want to find old movie locations and studios, movie stars' homes, and famous old Hollywood hot spots.

If you want to see what Hollywood looked like in its heyday, go to the soda fountain at On Location Hollywood shop and café. Here you'll find a miniature model of Hollywood in the 1940s, lots of Hollywood souvenirs to buy, and old-fashioned ice-cream sodas to drink.

In the courtyard of Mann's Chinese Theater, on Hollywood Boulevard, you will find the handprints and footprints of famous movie stars, together with their autographs, pressed into cement. Another favorite attraction of movie fans is the Walk of Fame at the corner of Hollywood and Vine, where there are over 1,800 names of famous Hollywood celebrities engraved in bronze stars set into the sidewalk.

Gulliver

T·R·A·V·E·L D·I·A·R·Y

I saw the movie star _____

in _____. If I could see a star

in person, I would like to see _____

and go _____ with him/her.

❖ ❖ ❖

If you just *have* to see your favorite star, your best chance is at the Hollywood Wax Museum, just two blocks from Mann's Chinese Theater. Here are dozens of actors and actresses—all made of wax.

In Beverly Hills, not too far out of Hollywood, is the world-renowned shopping area of Rodeo Drive. Within just a few blocks, people can buy fur coats, Rolls Royce cars, gold jewelry, perfume, handmade chocolates, and Italian ice cream. The street is lined with stores where thousands of dollars can be spent on a single piece of clothing.

Italian Ice Cream. Cone only $12.00

Did you know?

There are over 210 parks and playgrounds in Los Angeles.

■ ■ ■

Will Rogers Park has playgrounds, hiking trails, and the Will Rogers Museum.

■ ■ ■

Roxbury Park, in Beverly Hills, puts on children's theater throughout the summer.

■ ■ ■

Elysian Park, home of the Dodgers' baseball stadium, is right next to downtown and has playgrounds and hiking trails.

■ ■ ■

Barnsdall Park, on Hollywood Boulevard, has a junior arts-and-crafts center where kids can take classes in art and acting.

■ ■ ■

Did you visit any of these?

WESTWOOD

Sandwiched between Hollywood and Santa Monica, Westwood is "downtown" for the tens of thousands of students at the University of California, Los Angeles (known as UCLA). Westwood is famous for its trends. You'll find the latest fashions here—in clothes, haircuts, restaurants, ice cream parlors, movies. Westwood has more movie theaters in one area than any other place in L.A. On weekend evenings, some streets are closed to cars because the movie lines flow into the streets. Most new movies have their premieres here, so if you want to see the latest, visit Westwood.

SANTA MONICA BEACH

Up and down the Greater L.A. coastline, from Malibu to Long Beach, there are clean silver-gray beaches where you can build castles in the sand and play in the cool waves. Santa Monica Beach, west of downtown and Hollywood, is one of L.A.'s most popular beaches.

Years ago, vacationers liked to come here to get away from the city. They would pitch tents in the canyons and hike down to the water for a swim. Now the city of Santa Monica reaches right to the edge of the cliffs overlooking the beach. Main Street (closed to cars) is a busy and popular shopping mall. Palisades Park, a grassy strip popular for picnics and jogging, is all that's left of the open land.

The beach is long and wide here. There are special areas for swimmers, surfers, and boogie-boarders. If you don't want to get wet, you can rent a bike or roller skates, and roll down the miles of sidewalk along the beach.

If you get tired of the sand and sea, visit the Santa Monica Pier. There are bumper cars to ride and a penny arcade filled with the smells of popcorn, cotton candy, and corn dogs. At the end of the pier, you can rent gear and go fishing. On weekends the beautifully painted 70-year-old carousel is open, and you can ride one of its 46 prancing wooden horses.

SPRUCE GOOSE AND QUEEN MARY

About an hour down the coast from Los Angeles, in the harbor city of Long Beach, you can visit the biggest airplane and ocean liner you will probably ever see.

The *Spruce Goose* is the largest airplane ever built. Its wings are wider than a football field, and its tail is taller than an 8-story building. You can look inside the cockpit (where the pilot sat) and the cargo bay, which is big enough for 750 people or 8 helicopters!

The *Queen Mary* is the biggest ocean liner afloat. You can walk all over the ship and look at many of its rooms, including the room where the gigantic engines are. The *Queen Mary* now has a theater, hotel, disco, restaurants, and shops inside it.

Did you know?

The *Spruce Goose* was built by the billionaire Howard Hughes. He was the pilot for its one brief flight, on November 2, 1947. It lasted just one minute, and the plane never got more than 70 feet in the air. The *Spruce Goose* was a seaplane.

■ ■ ■

The *Queen Mary* has enough beds to sleep about 3,000 people.

Will We Have Any Fun?

DISNEYLAND

Believe it or not, Disneyland is known by more people around the world than any other place in the United States. Ask people what's in California, and most will answer, "Disneyland."

There is so much to do here that you could spend all day and still have more to come back and see the day after—but you'll probably be too tired for another trip!

Can you imagine visiting 7 different foreign lands without ever leaving Southern California? Take a trip to the Magic Kingdom of Disneyland in Orange County, just 27 miles southeast of downtown Los Angeles. The park is divided into 7 different sections, each with its own special theme. If you don't want to walk, there's a railroad to take you around the park.

Did you know?

Walt Disney grew up on a farm in Missouri. He left at the age of 16 to join the Red Cross.

■ ■ ■

Disneyland first opened in 1955.

■ ■ ■

Walt Disney first produced the Mickey Mouse cartoon in his studio in 1928.

■ ■ ■

There are over 800 species of plants from 40 nations in Disneyland.

■ ■ ■

Some of the trees in Storybook Land are 150 years old and only a foot tall.

You start your trip on Main Street, U.S.A., where everything looks like America did way before you or your parents were born, around the year 1900.

In Adventureland, you will visit exotic regions of Asia, Africa, and the South Pacific. Here you can take a jungle cruise. In the Enchanted Tiki Room, you will hear birds talking in 4 different languages. From Adventureland, step into Bear Country. Don't miss the Country Bear Jamboree here. The musical stories change, but the mechanical bears—along with a moose, a buffalo, a stag, a skunk, and an octopus—are always there to dance and sing you a song.

Fantasyland is the place where storybooks come alive. You'll be able to visit the scenes of many of your favorite Disney stories, fly through the air with Peter Pan, and float down a water canal through the miniature foreign countries of It's a Small World.

New Orleans Square, the home of the Haunted Mansion and Pirates of the Caribbean, is awaiting your arrival. Be careful—the ghosts and pirates are out to get you here! After you've been scared half to death, you'll be ready to try one of the many good restaurants in the park.

Did you know?

About 10 million people visit Disneyland every year and eat over 4,500,000 hamburgers.

If you're looking into the future, Tomorrowland will be the next stopover in your travels. Besides exploring Space Mountain, be sure to visit the two newest attractions: *Captain EO,* starring Michael Jackson, and Star Tours, an adventure through space. Another fun

---

DISNEYLAND SCRAMBLE

Disneyland is a big place, and I've gotten lost. Please unscramble the Disney characters below and fit them into the crossword puzzle to figure out where I am.

(Answers on page 129)

WHONIWEST   ___ ___ ___ ___ ___ ___ ___ ___ ___

IMBAB   ___ ___ ___ ___ ___

TUOPL   ___ ___ ___ ___ ___

HTEEPNHONIWIO   ___ ___ ___ ___ ___ ___ ___ ___ ___ ___ ___ ___ ___

APTREEPM   ___ ___ ___ ___ ___ ___ ___ ___

SMEOCYKIEMU   ___ ___ ___ ___ ___ ___ ___ ___ ___ ___

CDLOADUDNK   ___ ___ ___ ___ ___ ___ ___ ___ ___

OMDUB   ___ ___ ___ ___ ___

THERDMATA   ___ ___ ___ ___ ___ ___ ___ ___

LANDRECILE   ___ ___ ___ ___ ___ ___ ___ ___ ___ ___

SHALFUB   ___ ___ ___ ___ ___ ___ ___

GRETGI   ___ ___ ___ ___ ___ ___

FOYGO   ___ ___ ___ ___ ___

NOMESEIMNUI   ___ ___ ___ ___ ___ ___ ___ ___ ___ ___ ___

thing to see here is a motion picture shown on screens that circle all the way around you.

Your trip wouldn't be complete without turning the clock back to the Old West in Frontierland. Here you'll ride the railroad past Big Thunder Ranch, where you can see a blacksmith's forge and a harness-making shop, draft horses in corrals, and even barnyard animals that you can pet. If you get hungry, there's a barbecue area where you can enjoy food cooked on an open-air grill and served right from a chuck wagon.

If you stay until dark, you can see fireworks and different electric-light parades during special seasons. From Thanksgiving through Christmas, the whole of the Magic Kingdom is transformed into a winter wonderland. There are special musical shows, including the Very Merry Christmas Parade. And best of all, right in the middle of Town Square stands a 60-foot-tall Christmas tree decorated with 3,000 sparkling lights.

KNOTT'S BERRY FARM

The nation's oldest amusement theme park is located in Buena Park, just 30 minutes south of Los Angeles and only 10 minutes from Disneyland. Knott's Berry Farm offers over 165 rides, attractions, live shows, restaurants, and shops on its 150 acres.

There are five different sections to explore. Ghost Town is an authentic reproduction of an 1880s California mining town. Here you'll be able to pan for *real* gold, ride in an authentic stagecoach, and sail down a 70-foot mountain in a hollowed-out log. Many of Ghost Town's buildings were moved here from actual desert towns long since deserted, and a walk through the streets tells interesting tales of the Old West. You may want to stop to see the *Wild West*

Stunt Show, an old-time melodrama at the Bird Cage Theatre, or a cancan in the Calico Saloon. If you love video and pinball games, you'll go wild in the Buffalo Nickel Arcade. And don't miss a ride on the original Denver–Rio Grande train, which is pulled by Red Cliff Engine Number 41.

When you've finished exploring the Old West, early Spanish California awaits in Fiesta Village. Here you'll be able to eat Mexican food, hear the music of the mariachi bands, and buy lots of souvenirs. Here, too, you'll find Montezooma's Revenge, a frighteningly fun roller coaster.

If you're ready to try some more thrills, The Roaring '20s is the place to go. It looks just like California amusement parks did in the 1920s. You can play

Did you know?

The 3,082 bottles that make up the Bottle House face inward so they won't whistle when the wind blows.

games in the penny arcade, watch old shows in the Toyota Good Time Theatre, and see water shows in the aquatic arena in the Pacific Pavilion. The rides here, however, are pure 1980s—the Corkscrew is the very first upside-down roller coaster, and there's even a 20-story Parachute Sky Jump. And don't miss Kingdom of the Dinosaurs, where you can travel back

RIDDLE-ME-THIS

They love me at Knott's Berry Farm. In fact, you can find my picture on lots of the gifts and souvenirs. Who am I? I'll give you a clue. My name is hidden in this crossword puzzle.

1. _ _ _ _ _ _ _ Park, California

2. Walter and _ _ _ _ _ _ _ _ _ Knott

3. _ _ _ _ _ _ _ _ _ Fantasy on Parade

4. _ _ _ _ _ _ Town

5. _ _ _ _ _ _ _ –Rio Grande train

6. Calico _ _ _ _ _ _

7. _ _ _ _ _ _ _ _ Nickel Arcade

8. Red Cliff _ _ _ _ _ _ Number 41

9. Montezuma's _ _ _ _ _ _ _

10. Toyota Good Time _ _ _ _ _ _ _

11. Camp _ _ _ _ _ _

(Answers on page 129)

in time to the age of huge prehistoric reptiles. The special effects are great!

Camp Snoopy is the home of the *Peanuts* cartoon family. You can wander across bridges suspended between mountain peaks and among rushing waterfalls. Then see a show of "Snoopy Animal Friends"—a red-tailed hawk, a raccoon, an opossum, and even a gray wolf. There's a Paddle Wheel Steamer that's fun to take across the lake.

There's an exciting new area of Knott's Berry Farm. It's called Wild Water Wilderness, and it looks just like a national park during the turn of the century. Here you'll discover nature paths, a ranger station, and Bigfoot Rapids, a thrilling new white-water rafting journey past cascading waterfalls, geysers, and wooded shores. Don't expect to stay dry on this one!

MAGIC MOUNTAIN

Six Flags Magic Mountain is 260 acres of fun located north of Los Angeles on Interstate 5.

There are some great roller coasters here. The Shockwave drops you 85 feet at speeds of up to 55 miles per hour, and then zooms up to 66 feet—all while you're standing. The wooden Colossus speeds two miles through steep hills, the steel Revolution does a full loop, and the Goldrusher takes you back to the days of mining trains. The newest roller coaster, Ninja, is suspended from an overhead track. Not only does it race at lightning speed, it swings from side to side! For more thrills, you can ride a raft down a

Did you know?

The Colossus is listed in the Guinness Book of World Records as the world's largest dual-track wooden roller coaster.

raging river, skydive, and feel what it's like to be weightless on a ride that looks like a pirate ship.

Bugs Bunny World is for all of you kids 56 inches (that's 4 feet 8 inches) and under. The rides include Baron von Fudd Flyers, the Wile E. Coyote Coaster, and Road Runner Racers. There's a petting zoo with 55 different kinds of birds and animals. Don't forget to say hi to your Looney Tunes friends, Bugs, Daffy, and Sylvester.

Spillikin Handcrafters Junction lets you see what craftsmen of 100 years ago did. Candlemakers, broom-makers, and sign-makers show you their skills. Then there are all the shops to visit. The grounds are planted with some 11,000 trees, and there's even a Japanese garden. All types of music fill the park, from

rock to Dixieland. And if you love to eat, there's plenty of food, too.

When it's time to sit back and relax for a while, you may want to watch the Dolphin and Sea Lion Show or the high diving at the Aqua Theatre, or the Animal Chatter Show at the Pavilion, where you'll be able to both see and touch the animals, or Bugs Bunny's Wonder Circus. And in July and August you can watch a spectacular fireworks display over Mystic Lake.

RAGING WATERS

If you love water sports but aren't quite ready to ride a surfboard in the ocean, try visiting Raging Waters in San Dimas, the largest water theme park west of the Mississippi.

Here you can safely ride a water slide over treetops and through underground tunnels, or shoot down a river under a waterfall and into whirlpools on a rubber tube. And for the really brave, there are two 80-foot dive slides.

Did you know?

There's enough water in the Raging Waters Wave Cove to fill 25,000 bathtubs.

T·R·A·V·E·L D·I·A·R·Y

I rode _____ rides at _____.

I really liked the _____ because _____

_____. I didn't like the _____

_____.

because it _____

The amusement parks in Southern California are a lot of fun.

I visited:

_____ Disneyland   _____ Knott's Berry Farm

_____ Magic Mountain   _____ Raging Waters

❖ ❖ ❖

There's also plenty for small kids, too. They can splash and slide in their own waterfalls, slideways, and waterspouts. When you've worked up an appetite, there's everything from pizza to chicken to eat, or you can have your own picnic and barbecue.

NBC STUDIO TOUR

Put yourself in the studio seat and see how you'd look on television. The 75-minute tour gives you a view of what's happening the day you're there. You will also be able to see yourself on camera, attend a video make-up demonstration, see how a set is constructed, and visit the wardrobe area. If you plan your trip far enough in advance, you can request tickets to a recording of a live NBC-TV show.

GOT THE PICTURE?

Gulliver Productions has just hired you as the official set designer. You design the set for this Wild West show. (Example on page 130)

Did you know?

The site of Universal Studios used to be a chicken ranch. In fact, back in 1915, eggs were sold at the end of each tour.

Two new attractions will certainly catch your fancy—the special effects set, where you may be chosen to fly, and Tour Trivia, a special game of live and recorded fun.

UNIVERSAL STUDIOS TOUR

This is your chance to glimpse the world of television and motion picture make-believe.

Hop aboard the tram and be captured by a spaceship. Escape, and go behind the scenes to see how the special effects are done. You'll experience a flash flood, an earthquake, and the parting of the Red Sea. And you won't be able to avoid meeting King Kong—he weighs 6½ tons and is as tall as a 3-story building.

After the tour, take in any or all of the five 15-minute shows. The newest one is the Miami Vice Action Spectacular, an exciting display of stunts and special effects used in the popular TV show. Dragons and fireballs startle the crowd in the *Adventures of Conan*.

T·R·A·V·E·L D·I·A·R·Y

My favorite movie of all time is _____.

My favorite TV show is _____,

and my favorite actor/actress is _____.

because _____

I've seen a lot here in Los Angeles. I still want to see
_____ if I come back.

Some places I went in L.A. that weren't in this book were
_____.

_____

❖ ❖ ❖

See the best of the cowboy stunts at the *Western Stunt Show,* or join the crew of the starship *Enterprise* at *Star Trek Adventure.* For you animal lovers, there's the *Animal Actors Show,* where you can see animals perform. This is a great place to see a movie, too. The new Universal City cinemas, Cineplex Odeon, offer a choice of 18 different movies.

Outside Los Angeles

Did you know?

If you take a boat ride after dark, you can see flying fish off the coast of the island. Some fly out of the water as far as 75 yards.

A lot of people think that Southern California is one big city. That's because most people just see San Diego or Los Angeles. But there are some great wilderness trips just a few hours away: Mountains, deserts, forests, and hot springs are east of L.A., and there's an island off the coast of Long Beach.

CATALINA ISLAND

Just a 22-mile boat ride from Long Beach is Santa Catalina Island. Here you can take a tour on a bus or a glass-bottom boat. For some exercise, rent a bike, boat, inner tube, kayak, or snorkel, and enjoy the island park, zoo, and underwater gardens.

ANZA BORREGO DESERT STATE PARK

Anza Borrego is just three hours east of Los Angeles or San Diego. It is the largest state park in the United States—a half-million acres!—and it's hot, dry, and quiet. When the sun goes down, the desert animals come out

After the first rain of spring, the desert flowers bloom, and people from the cities drive out by the thousands to enjoy the beautiful landscape. Color this springtime desert landscape.

to play. On your way to L.A. from the east, you might drive through Joshua Tree National Monument, another desert-type park. This one, though, has tall funny-shaped trees that look like people with their hands over their heads, as if someone had yelled, "Stick 'em up."

Did you know?

A Joshua tree isn't really a tree at all. It's a big cactus with no leaves.

Did you know?

The Morongo Indian Reservation is just west of Palm Springs and has a good collection of Indian artifacts on display.

PALM SPRINGS

Palm Springs is a desert town that was first settled by Indians who found freshwater springs there. Most people come to play golf, tennis, or sit by the swimming pool in the dry, hot, clean air. Just out of town there's a tramway you can ride 2.5 miles to the top of the San Jacinto Mountains. In just twenty minutes it takes you from desert sand to mountain snow, where you can hike or go cross-country skiing.

IDYLLWILD

Idyllwild is a village in the mountains between the deserts and Los Angeles. It's a popular place to escape from the heat in the summer; in the winter it's a snow playground. There are mountain trails to hike all year round, and when the weather permits, you can hike all the way to the top of Mount San Jacinto. If you're not a hiker, there are lots of shops to visit—including a great candy shop and bakery.

DEATH VALLEY

Death Valley is a desert like no other. Encircled by 10,000-foot-high mountains, it can reach temperatures as high as 134 degrees—that's the record for Death Valley. You will be amazed at the beautiful colors of the rocks—greens, purples, yellows, and reds. They're so wonderfully strange that you might think you're on another planet. Look also for coyotes, foxes, and roadrunners; you'll see them in the cool mornings and evenings.

Did you know?

Mount Whitney—of the Sierra Nevada range—at 14,494 feet is the tallest peak in the continental U.S. It is only 60 miles from the lowest point in North America, Death Valley, at 282 feet below sea level.

■ ■ ■

It only rains about 2 inches a year in Death Valley.

75

S·A·N D·I·E·G·O

Most travelers visit San Diego for two reasons: to see the animals and to play at the beach. San Diego has the best of both, and the perfect weather lets you enjoy them all year round.

Even though San Diego is the eighth-largest city in the United States, it's easy to find your way around. Highway 5 runs from north to south, and Highway 8 runs from east to west. Both cross straight through San Diego. Almost everything you will want to see here is a short trip off one of these major roads.

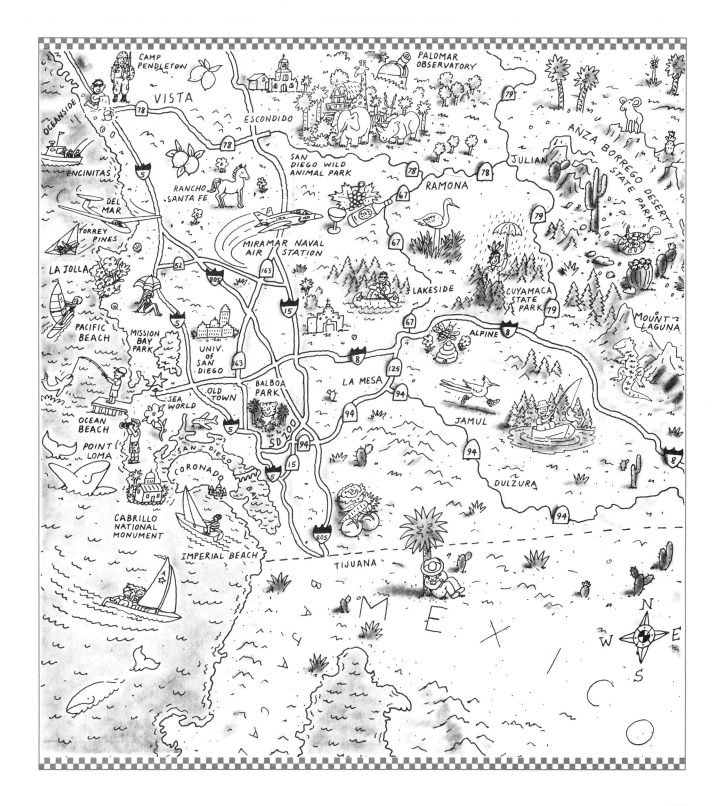

It's fun to send postcards to friends while you're away. It's also fun to send postcards to yourself. Write a postcard to yourself in the space provided below.

Make a list of people you want to send postcards to.

_____   _____

_____   _____

_____   _____

To:

Are There Any Animals?

THE SAN DIEGO ZOO

The San Diego Zoo is one of the world's great zoos—and one of the largest. It spreads out over 100 acres of canyons and mesas in Balboa Park, providing plenty of room for the more than 3,000 animals and 5,000 kinds of plants here.

Many of the animals are out in the open (no cages!), with only a moat or trench separating them from you. Birds are in cages big enough for people to walk through. Hummingbirds zoom like miniature jet-propelled missiles right toward you. Luckily, they have good brakes! They stop and hover at the tip of your nose—just as curious about you as you are about them!

Try the three-mile guided bus tour through the zoo. It takes only 40 minutes, and you'll see lots of the larger animals—hippos, elephants, bears, giraffes, and antelope—and hear some interesting facts and silly

Did you know?

The plants growing at the San Diego Zoo are now worth more than the animals.

■ ■ ■

A *mesa* (MAY-sah) is a hill with a flat top.

■ ■ ■

A moat is just a deep trench usually filled with water.

The zookeeper has lined up the food for the animals according to their place in the alphabet. But the animals are not lined up properly. Place the names of the animals in alphabetical order by putting numbers next to them in the order that they should appear, so that the zookeeper can give them the proper food.

_____ dingo   _____ giraffe

_____ condor   _____ black bear

_____ elephant   _____ tiger

_____ gorilla   _____ otter

_____ hedgehog   _____ alligator

_____ pelican   _____ kangaroo

_____ fox   _____ anteater

_____ owl   _____ zebra

_____ bison   _____ spider monkey

_____ panda   _____ platypus

_____ jaguar   _____ coyote

(Answer on page 130)

Did you know?

Koalas are close cousins of the kangaroo. They're not bears!

■ ■ ■

Koalas eat mostly eucalyptus leaves. The leaves are not a great source of energy, so the koalas move very slowly, usually just from one bunch of leaves to another.

stories about them. You can always go back later on foot if you want a closer look.

The park is north of downtown San Diego, and if you ride Skyfari—the colorful chairs that cross over the zoo on cables high in the air—you can look out over the skyscrapers to San Diego Bay and the Pacific Ocean beyond.

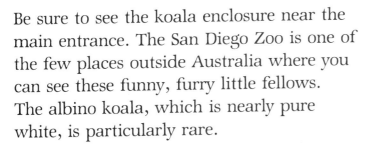

Be sure to see the koala enclosure near the main entrance. The San Diego Zoo is one of the few places outside Australia where you can see these funny, furry little fellows. The albino koala, which is nearly pure white, is particularly rare.

You'll also want to visit the Children's Zoo and watch the baby animals being fed and cared for. You can pet guinea pigs, rabbits, baby goats, sheep, and even a porcupine.

The otters in the Children's Zoo are very playful. You can watch them from outside or go into the cave and watch them swim underwater.

Don't miss the Reptile House. It's full of all kinds of lizards and snakes—including rattlesnakes, pythons, and cobras.

Did you bring a camera with you? If you did, don't miss getting a shot of your favorite animal.

You'll need at least a full day for all the things there are to do at this zoo. Comfortable shoes are really important because you'll probably be on your feet—unless you're riding on a bus, a camel, or an elephant!

SAN DIEGO WILD ANIMAL PARK

The Wild Animal Park, near the town of Escondido (about a 45-minute drive northeast of San Diego), covers 1,800 acres of land very much like the wild plains, veldts, and savannahs of Africa and India.

T·R·A·V·E·L D·I·A·R·Y

My favorite animal is the _____ because
_____ .
_____ .
It looks like _____
Some of the most unusual animals I saw were _____
_____ .
_____
If I could take an animal home from the zoo with me, I'd
choose a/an _____ because _____
_____
If I could be any kind of animal I wanted, I would be a/an ____
_____ and my name would be _____ .

❖ ❖ ❖

Some 3,500 animals, including ostriches, rhinoceroses, giraffes, wildcats, zebras, elephants, and antelope roam here freely. You can watch the animals during a 60-minute ride on the monorail that encircles the

Did you know?

The people at the San Diego Wild Animal Park work hard to preserve endangered animal species. They find and incubate the eggs of the California condor a huge black bird with an orange neck and head and a 10-foot wingspan, which is becoming more and more rare.

park. Then you'll probably want to hike along the trails to get a different, perhaps closer, look at the animals. The park also has an animal care center and an area where you can pet some of the less ferocious beasts. If you didn't get a chance at the zoo, there are also elephants and camels to ride here. And don't miss the animal shows. Just about every hour, trainers show off the talents of birds, elephants, and other assorted creatures.

SEA WORLD

Are you ready for a meeting with over 400 penguins in their native habitat? How about getting splashed by a killer whale? Or feeding lunch to a walrus? Or

perhaps you'd like to pet a dolphin? All of this and much more awaits you at Sea World on the south shore of Mission Bay.

You'll need to keep a tight schedule to see all of the shows and exhibits in one day. One of the sights you especially won't want to miss is Shamu, a 2-ton killer whale who stars in his own show, with able help from his human trainers. Be careful where you sit, because the first 6 rows of the stadium often get very wet when Shamu leaps and dives.

HIDDEN ANIMALS

The animals are hiding. See if you can find (and color) the
animals from the list below.

penguin	dolphin	shark	starfish
walrus	whale	seal	clam

(Answer on page 130)

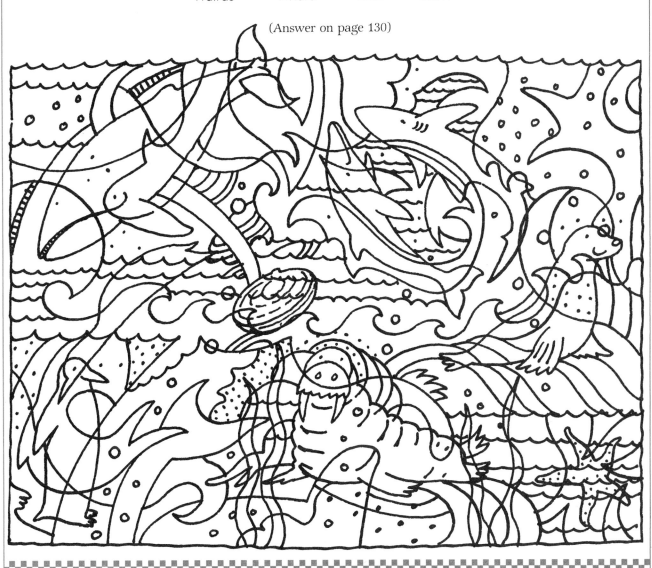

For an exciting trip to the Antarctic, visit the Penguin Encounter. A moving sidewalk carries you alongside snowcapped peaks and icy seawater, where the penguins waddle along in the snow and glide gracefully in the water. Hundreds of eggs have hatched since the exhibit was opened, so you may get to see a baby penguin or two, usually shown on TV from the nursery. Other land and shore birds—including the puffins, whose antics are often very funny to watch—are also located in the exhibit.

Did you know?

Penguins have feathers that act like a waterproof coat. They lost their ability to fly millions of years ago. Their wings turned into flippers—now penguins "fly" under water.

■ ■ ■

A penguin colony is called a *rookery*.

Of the four major aquariums located throughout Sea World, none is more awesome than the 400,000-gallon Shark Exhibit. Among the inhabitants, you'll see bull, lemon, blacktip, and sand tiger sharks, one of which is nearly 9 feet long! On your way out of the exhibit, make sure you stop at the model of the jaw structure of the prehistoric ancestor of the Great White sharks. You'll feel small in comparison.

You won't want to miss the Seal and Otter Show, a whodunit set in a spooky, kooky castle; the New Friends Dolphin and Whale Show in which these marine mammals perform all sorts of aerial acrobatics; or the petting pool, where you can feed and pet both white-sided dolphins and pilot whales.

For a break from the animals, visit Cap'N Kids World, a 2-acre play area featuring the Fishnet Climb, a unique jungle gym; the Ball Crawl—a tank full of colored plastic balls that you can "swim" in; the King of the Wave, a 9-foot vinyl wave for climbing; and the Swashbuckler's Swing. Only persons 37 to 61 inches in height (or roughly 3 to 13 years old) can get in, so while you visit Cap'N Kids World, the tall people traveling with you may want to visit the Sparkletts Water Fantasy show or check out the view of San Diego from the top of the 340-foot Sky Tower.

Did you know?

Seals have holes in their heads for ears. Sea lions have ear flaps, like us.

If the big whales make you feel small, take a walk through the new Places of Learning here at Sea World. There are 15 famous children's books so big that you'll feel like you're in a fairy tale yourself. Each book is 4 feet high and 6 feet wide! Near the books is a 40-foot chessboard with playing pieces 3 to 5 feet tall, and a map of the United States so big that you can walk around the states, crossing rivers, highways, and cities with each step. See if you can find the city where you were born. And don't miss the Parent's Store while you're here. It's where you take your parents to buy books, games, toys, maps, and other things made especially for kids.

Connect the dots to see what Gulliver is doing.

(Answer on page 130)

Several of the smaller exhibits are worth your time. See the California sea otters, who are often on their backs eating shellfish; the California tide pool, where you can pick up and examine a starfish; and the Japanese Village, where pearl divers bring up oysters *guaranteed* to have a pearl. During the summer and holidays, special shows are offered in the evenings till 11:00 P.M., along with fireworks, music, and other entertainments.

SCRIPPS AQUARIUM

Up the coast from Sea World, just north of downtown La Jolla, the Scripps Aquarium and Museum houses a unique collection of sea life from San Diego, the Sea of Cortez (just south of California, in Mexico), and the Pacific coral reefs. There are over 1,500 sea animals in some 22 tanks, as well as an onshore tide pool containing many animals in their natural habitat. The sea horses, sea stars (looking like masses of coiled snakes), and hermit crabs are some of the more eye-catching species on display. Special activities, including beach walks, whale-watching tours, and tips on aquarium care, are offered throughout the year. Classes in marine biology are offered each summer to kids of all ages.

What's That?

BALBOA PARK

Right in the heart of San Diego is one of the oldest and largest city parks in the United States. Here you'll be able to find almost any cultural or recreational activity: museums, theaters, sports facilities, and even a zoo.

Balboa Park, once just sagebrush and cactus, now is covered with beautiful plants from all over the world. Most of the plants are from Australia, which has weather like Southern California's. But there are also trees and plants from China, Japan, Africa, and South America. There is something in this park for everyone. You can play outside on one of the many lawns, visit all kinds of museums, see a play, or visit the zoo.

Did you know?

Two world fairs were held at Balboa Park: the Panama–California Exposition of 1915–16 and the California Pacific International Exposition of 1935–36.

Have you seen enough animals yet? No? Then let's start our tour of Balboa Park at the **Natural History Museum.** Here you will see animals that aren't alive in any zoo or aquarium. This museum contains stuffed rare and extinct animals, along with plants and rocks that are native to the southwest United States and northern Mexico. And if you like dinosaurs, this is the place to be. There are full-size skeletons of dinosaurs, and stories of how they lived millions of years ago.

Just across the square—past the round fountain, jugglers, and breakdancers—is the **Reuben H. Fleet Space Theater and Science Center.** This isn't your ordinary movie theater. The special camera and 152 speakers make you feel like you are really traveling in

ANIMAL COUSINS

Nine thousand to 40,000 years ago, there were many animals living in Southern California, such as

antique bison
American mastodon
western horse
sabertooth cat
dire wolf
sloth
American lion
imperial mammoth
American camel
merriam teraform (bird)
short-faced bear

Can you guess which ones still have relatives in the United States today?

(Answer on page 130)

a spaceship or time machine. In the Science Center, you can have fun playing with 50 exhibits that help you figure out many of the mysteries of the world— which is what science is all about. There's an antigravity mirror that makes it look like you're lifting your feet off the ground or makes your head disappear, and an exhibit that shows you how invisible particles from outer space are made visible in a cloud chamber.

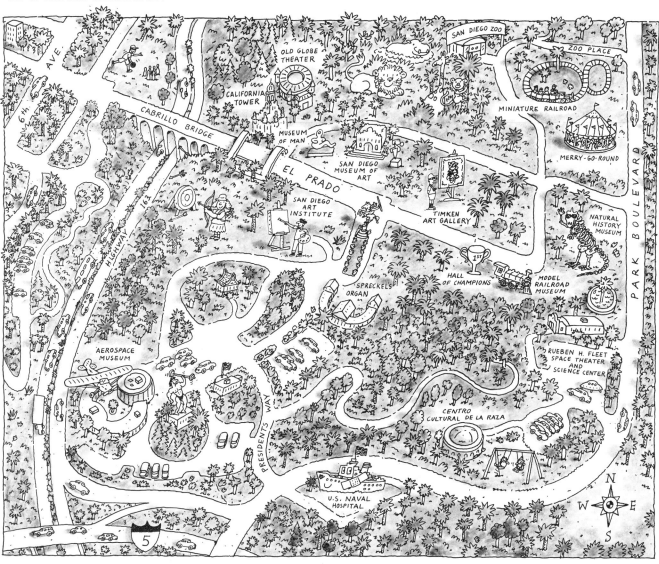

If you walk down the long wide sidewalk from these museums, you can find signs that lead to the **Hall of Champions.** If you're a sports fan, you will love this museum. It is filled with videos, pictures, uniforms, medals, and equipment from famous star athletes from San Diego. You can walk on real Astroturf and ask a computer for Padres baseball facts.

The Hall of Champions includes all major sports, plus some of San Diego's favorites—surfing, rowing, and bicycling. A favorite of kids is the sports "bloopers" films full of their favorite sports stars making funny mistakes in their games.

Did you know?

Greg Louganis, the U.S. and world champion diver, is from San Diego.

T·R·A·V·E·L D·I·A·R·Y

My favorite sports team is _____.

They are from _____.

and they play _____,

My favorite sports star is _____.

who is a _____ for _____

❖ ❖ ❖

93

If you're crazy about railroads, don't miss the **Model Railroad Museum,** next to the Hall of Champions. There are four different sizes of models here, on tracks that wind through replicas of San Diego and the Old West.

For those who like art, the **San Diego Museum of Art** has a collection of beautiful paintings, pottery, and sculpture from ancient Egypt through modern times. Next door is the **Timken Art Gallery,** which is full of famous European and American paintings. Outside the main art museum, enclosed within a high iron fence, is yet another kind of art museum—a sculpture garden.

The wooden buildings behind the sculpture garden are built to look like the theaters did in England some 400 years ago. That's when William Shakespeare's plays were performed in a London theater called the Old Globe. People have been watching them ever since. Balboa Park's **Old Globe Theatre** puts on Shakespearean plays every summer, as well as other plays, both new and old, throughout the year. The dancers you often see outside the theater on weekends are dressed in costumes of Shakespeare's time.

Did you know?

Shakespeare wrote approximately three dozen plays, many of them masterpieces. He is said by many to be the greatest writer who ever lived.

The park has four other theaters for live performances, including a Puppet Theater, and a Junior Theater, where all the parts are played by young people.

The museum past the Old Globe and just before you cross Cabrillo Bridge is the **Museum of Man.** Here you can see exhibits showing native people and cultures of the western Americas—that's western parts of South America, Central America, and North America—from ancient times to the present. Look for the live demonstrations of people weaving blankets and making tortillas by hand.

MUSEUM HUNT

Gulliver is organizing a scavenger hunt. Draw a line from the items on his list to the museums where they can most likely be found.

cloud chamber   Natural History Museum

dinosaur skeleton   Reuben H. Fleet Space Theater
                                       and Science Center
sculpture
                                  Hall of Champions
Padre uniform
                                  San Diego Museum of Art
arrowhead
                                  Museum of Man
piñata
                                  Aerospace Museum
hot-air balloon
                                  Centro Cultural de la Raza

(Answer on page 131)

A short walk to the end of the Pan-American Plaza takes you to the tall, round **Aerospace Museum and International Aerospace Hall of Fame.** The museum has over 55 aircraft. You will see almost every kind of plane ever made, from the first ones constructed with paper and wood to modern spacecraft. There is also a collection of warplanes, from the old bombers of World War I to the jet fighters of today. The hall is set up so you walk through time, from the hot-air balloon to space capsules.

At the **Centro Cultural de la Raza** you can see arts and crafts made by present-day Indians, Mexicans, and Chicanos (Americans of Mexican descent). You can't miss the building—it's round and covered with a bright painting.

There is hardly a day in the whole year when the weather isn't right for a day outside in Balboa Park. Along the sidewalks are magicians, jugglers, acrobats,

96

and musicians to entertain you. Near the zoo there is a 58-passenger miniature train and a Victorian merry-go-round that are open every day in the summer, and on weekends and holidays the rest of the year. There are two kids' playgrounds, with swings and jungle gyms, and acres of open grass for running, playing ball, throwing a Frisbee®, or setting out a picnic. Across the Cabrillo Bridge, along Fifth Avenue, you can even rent bicycles and roller skates to use in the park.

Did you know?

The miniature train next to the zoo is one-fifth the size of a regular locomotive.

T·R·A·V·E·L D·I·A·R·Y

Of all the museums I visited on this trip, I like the _____ _____ best. It's full of _____. The best thing about it is _____ If I could have my own museum, I would call it _____, and inside I would have a collection of _____.

❖ ❖ ❖

SAN DIEGO BAY

The biggest bay in San Diego is by the airport and downtown. Not only are there big sailing and fishing boats, but this bay is so deep and wide that the huge Navy aircraft carriers can also come here—and they are as long as three football fields. On one of the many boats docked at the Embarcadero, you can take a tour of the bay and get a great view of all the ships and the downtown area.

Did you know?

San Diego is one of the three largest Navy complexes in the world. It is home port for over 100 ships.

NAUTICAL MUSEUMS

Sitting right in San Diego Bay at the end of Broadway, downtown's main street, are three more museums you'll want to visit. These are floating museums: old ships restored so you can see the way ships used to look. The one with the three tall masts is the *Star of India*, a sailing ship that's over 100 years old. It once carried cargo all the way from England to New Zealand. The *Medea* is a very fancy yacht that's over 80 years old. It was built to run on steam power and is made of beautiful wood. The first owner had it made to take his friends on hunting and fishing trips. Docked nearby is an old ferryboat, the *Berkeley*. It ferried passengers across San Francisco Bay before there were any bridges. Just last year, a ferry line from the Broadway Pier to Coronado Island was reopened, so you can go across the bay the same way people crossed before the Coronado Bridge was built.

Did you know?

The *Star of India*, built in 1863, made 21 trips around the world and is the oldest merchant vessel afloat.

■ ■ ■

The *Berkeley* helped in the evacuation of San Francisco following the earthquake and fire of 1906.

T·R·A·V·E·L D·I·A·R·Y

I've been on a _____ boat before. If I went on a boat trip, I would go on a _____ and visit _____. In San Diego I've seen _____ boats. The biggest I saw was a _____. The smallest was a _____.

❖ ❖ ❖

Identify each boat with its proper name from the list
below by writing it on the first line beneath the picture.
Use the second line to give the boat its own personal
name. See example:

rowboat

sailboat

battleship

ocean liner

paddleboat

_____rowboat_____

_____*Jennie, Too*_____

_____

_____

_____

_____

_____

_____

_____

_____

(Answers on page 131)

CORONADO ISLAND

The island in the middle of San Diego Bay isn't really an island. When you drive across the high blue curving bridge to visit Coronado, you can see the strip of sand that connects it to land in the south just before Mexico. As you start to cross the bridge, take a look at the colorful murals painted on the pillars of the entrance ramp. Many children helped the artists paint the murals of this famous park, known as Chicano Park.

The beach on Coronado is very wide. It's quite a hike through the sand from the street to the ocean, but you will have lots of room to play once you get there. The enormous white building with the round pointed tower and red roof is the Hotel del Coronado. It once was the only building on the island, and all around it were tents where people on vacation camped at the beach.

Did you know?

The Coronado Bridge is 2.2 miles long. The high curve design allows very tall ships to pass underneath. It is 246 feet above the water level of the bay.

Did you know?

The Hotel Del, as it is often called, is a favorite place of foreign royalty and famous movie stars. Ten presidents have also visited the hotel. And it was a regular hideaway for the author L. Frank Baum, who wrote *The Wizard of Oz*.

The hotel is one of the largest wooden buildings still standing in the United States. Built 100 years ago, it has 399 rooms, all with fireplaces. It was the first hotel in the world to have electric, instead of gas, lights. Thomas Edison, the famous inventor of the light bulb, came to supervise the installation.

Did you know?

The gray whales usually swim about half a mile from shore. You can see them when they surface and shoot a spray of water and air from their blowholes.

■ ■ ■

Off the coast of San Diego you can catch bass, bonita, barracuda, rock and ling cod, mackerel, halibut, yellowtail, albacore, and more.

SHELTER ISLAND

If you want to go for a long boat trip out into the ocean, take off from Shelter Island. Just past the airport, on your way to Point Loma, you'll find this little island surrounded by fishing boats. You can go whale-watching from December to March. The whales swim by on their way to the warm waters of Baja California. You can leave on a fishing trip from Shelter Island any time of the year, going for a half-day to the kelp beds or a full day to deeper water.

CABRILLO POINT

For a great view of San Diego, the bay, the ocean, and the southern coastline, take a drive past Shelter Island and out to Cabrillo Point. To get there, you'll have to go through Fort Rosecrans National Cemetery, where over 40,000 military men and women and their families are buried. Once out at the Point, make sure you walk to both sides to see the wonderful view.

Cabrillo National Monument, named for Juan Cabrillo, who first sailed into San Diego Harbor in 1542, is located at the very tip of Cabrillo Point. In the museum you can see models of Cabrillo, his fellow explorers, and their ships. From the museum patio you can look out over the North Island Navy airstrip, Coronado Island, and downtown San Diego. Don't miss the tour of the old lighthouse. It is restored to look just as it did when the watchman lived there about 130 years ago. This lighthouse, 462 feet above sea level, was often concealed by clouds—not good for a lighthouse—so a new one had to be built closer to the shore.

A bottle with a message in it has washed up on the shore. See if you can decode the message.

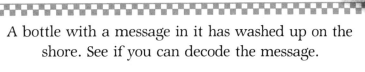  with the

C - ya!

(Answer on page 131)

Each year the California gray whales migrate over 4,000 miles from the Arctic Ocean near Alaska to Baja California to give birth to their young in warm water.

■ ■ ■

Baby whales are called *calves*.

Past the lighthouse is another viewpoint where you can look out over the Pacific Ocean. The little islands in the distance to the south are the Mexican islands called the Coronados. The city of Coronado was named after these islands. Down on the ocean side of the point are tide pools to visit. When the tide is low, you can view sea plants and animals swimming in tide pools in the rocks.

OLD TOWN

About 200 years after Cabrillo landed on Point Loma, the first European settlement on the west coast started in what we now call Old Town. Today, the little village is full of shops and restaurants, some of which are in restored buildings that were originally built over 200 years ago. Walk around Old Town and you will see part of San Diego history—from the missionaries to the pony express. The stores have a little of everything: toys, books, Mexican crafts, cowboy hats, art, clothes, candy, and much more. At Casa de Pedrorena, one of the many Mexican restaurants, you can buy Mexican pastries baked in a stone oven that's well over 100 years old.

Did you know?

You can see a 25-minute history show about the entire San Diego area at Seeley Stables.

The brightly painted wooden houses just behind Old Town were moved here from all over San Diego. They are part of Heritage Park and are from another time in San Diego history. These Victorian homes were originally built a little less than a 100 years ago but have since been remodeled into offices and shops.

The park above Old Town is Presidio Park, site of Fort Stockton and Father Serra's first mission. At the top of the park is the Serra Museum and a great view of Mission Bay and the Pacific Ocean.

MISSION BAY PARK

If you are a sailor you will want to visit Mission Bay, where you can rent a small sailboat (or a paddleboat if you can't sail) to cruise around the world's largest bay park. If you like to stay on shore, but want to cruise the bay, rent a bicycle or a pair of roller skates and roll on any part of the 13 miles of paths that circle the water. To get to the ocean from the bay, you just cross one of the main streets. There are only two blocks of houses and one street between the bay and the ocean. Beware! Runners and skateboard riders are everywhere.

Did you know?

You can visit the restored Whaley House in Old Town. It was built in 1857 out of handmade bricks and was a theater, store, church, and courthouse. Now it's a museum, and some people say it's haunted.

∎∎∎

The surfboards with sails are called *sailboards* or *windsurfers*. Experts ride them on the ocean waves just like a surfboard, but you'll see people riding them mostly on the smooth bay waters.

∎∎∎

There are over 300 miles of bike paths in San Diego, including the paths that circle Mission Bay.

∎∎∎

Kite flying is excellent around Mission Bay. One of the most popular spots is the park area right near Highway 5 and Sea World Drive.

PACIFIC BEACH AND MISSION BEACH

Now's your chance to play in the sand. Pacific and Mission beaches have perfect sand for building castles. In fact, throughout the summer there are sandcastle contests up and down the coast.

For brave and experienced swimmers, boogie-boards are for rent up and down Pacific and Mission beach. These boards are softer and shorter than surfboards. Look out in the ocean for the people riding waves lying down or kneeling on their boards. They're boogie-boarding! It's a lot easier and safer than surfing. The swimmers riding the waves with no boards are body-surfing. You have to kick your legs really hard to catch the waves without a board.

Did you know?

If you walk into the ocean in San Diego and swim due west you will land in Japan in about five months. (This is not advised!)

LA JOLLA COVE

North on Highway 5, near Scripps Aquarium, is La
Jolla Shores Beach. You can walk there from the
aquarium. Just around the corner (but too far to
walk) is the calm and colorful La Jolla Cove. If you

T·R·A·V·E·L D·I·A·R·Y

I _____ at the ocean. The water was _____.
If you get knocked down when swimming in the ocean, you
can get a mouthful of water. It tastes like _____.
Some of the things I did at the ocean:

___went surfing

___went swimming

___went bodysurfing

___chased seagulls

___went boogie-boarding

___walked

___jogged

___played Frisbee

___built a sandcastle

___got a sunburn

___got a tan

___collected shells

❖ ❖ ❖

like to snorkel, the cove is for you. There is a huge cave in the cliffs and a deep cove in the water that are favorite sites for hikers and divers to explore. You can put on a snorkel and mask, float with your face down, and see beautiful fish and plants just ten yards off the beach. This is also a great picnic site because there is plenty of grass right near the water. And on Sundays there are expert Frisbee® players who spin a disk like it's magic. If you have a Frisbee®, they'll give you free lessons.

CHILDREN'S MUSEUM OF SAN DIEGO

San Diego has a museum that's just for kids. East of Highway 5, inland from the Scripps Aquarium, in La Jolla Village Square shopping mall, is the Children's Museum of San Diego. Because it's in the middle of a huge shopping center, grown-ups can be sent out on their own to shop while you explore this special museum. You can pretend you are a doctor or a dentist in an office full of medical instruments. Or you can dress in costumes and perform on a stage, or be a newscaster on your own news program in the TV studio. There is an art studio full of things you can use to make your own art and a tunnel to walk through so you can feel what it's like to be blind.

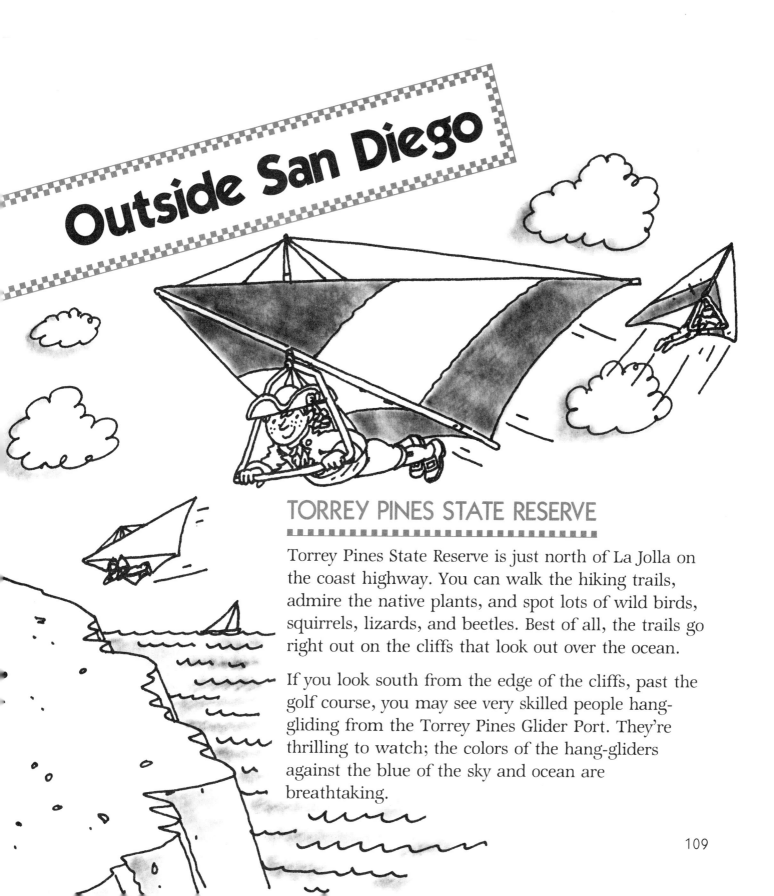

Outside San Diego

TORREY PINES STATE RESERVE

Torrey Pines State Reserve is just north of La Jolla on the coast highway. You can walk the hiking trails, admire the native plants, and spot lots of wild birds, squirrels, lizards, and beetles. Best of all, the trails go right out on the cliffs that look out over the ocean.

If you look south from the edge of the cliffs, past the golf course, you may see very skilled people hang-gliding from the Torrey Pines Glider Port. They're thrilling to watch; the colors of the hang-gliders against the blue of the sky and ocean are breathtaking.

WHAT'S WRONG WITH THIS PICTURE?

(Answers on page 131)

CUYAMACA STATE PARK

Cuyamaca (*koo-yah-MAH-ka*) State Park is just under an hour's drive northeast of San Diego on Route 79. Its name comes from the Kumeya Indian word that means "place-where-it-rains." Unlike the rest of Southern California, it gets from 30 to 35 inches of rain a year. There is a forest to hike through and a lake to fish in. There's also a great Indian museum by the park office that shows how the Indians once lived off the land here.

Past Cuyamaca Lake there is a road called the Sunrise Highway that leads up to the Laguna Mountain recreation area. The highway got its name from the incredible views east over the desert. Once you're up in the mountains, there are hiking trails and picnic grounds to enjoy.

T·R·A·V·E·L D·I·A·R·Y

My favorite thing in San Diego is _____.
If I come back here I will visit _____,
but I won't visit _____. I liked _____
_____ the best because _____

JULIAN

Julian is a small town with the Old West look. It's just a 60-mile drive from San Diego, not far from Cuyamaca. One hundred years ago miners struck gold here, and the town sprang up. You can see what the gold-rush town was like back then if you visit the Julian Museum. Julian also is the home of many festivals: an apple festival during the fall harvest season, and annual flower, weed, and fiddle contests during other seasons. Julian is always a good place to eat apple pie and drink apple cider.

LOOKING FOR GOLD

Julian is an old mining town. Help the kids pan for gold by finding the words listed below in the puzzle.

```
F  L  T  R  Z  A  O  L  R  D  S  T
R  G  O  L  D  D  U  S  T  M  A  L
I  N  T  D  R  G  G  F  Z  R  O  O
Z  I  D  G  B  N  U  G  G  E  T  R
G  O  L  R  U  Z  T  I  A  U  T  P
I  O  D  N  L  Y  F  A  B  Q  U  R
S  D  T  S  L  I  A  R  A  T  L  D
Y  R  A  N  I  U  G  G  R  S  T  U
R  I  N  G  O  T  S  I  L  V  B  O
N  R  E  I  N  G  F  O  I  A  G  T
```

GOLD DUST
NUGGET
BULLION
INGOT
BAR

(Answers on page 131)

South of the Border

If you want to go to another country while you're visiting Southern California, you can drive south on Interstate 5 to the U.S.–Mexico border. Or you can ride the San Diego trolley from downtown and walk across the border to the city of Tijuana. Tijuana has lots of fun places to shop and eat. If you want to learn about Mexico, visit the museum at the new Cultural Center near the huge modern shopping center, the Plaza Rio Tijuana. As you walk through the museum, the story of Mexico's history unfolds.

For sports fans, Tijuana has dog and horse races, bullfights, and the fastest game in the world—jai alai. This game is related to handball and is played inside a big sports palace in downtown Tijuana.

Did you know?

More people cross the border between Tijuana and San Diego each day than cross any other international border in the world.

■ ■ ■

Passports and visas are not necessary for U.S. citizens visiting Mexico for less than 72 hours and within 75 miles of the border.

Is That All?

Well, isn't Southern California a great place to visit? There is something here for everyone—parks, zoos, theaters, planetariums, sports, museums, beaches, mountains, and deserts.

You'll need to come back many times throughout your life to see it all. Reading up on where you want to go will help you enjoy your trips. And your travel journal will help you remember what to tell your friends about when you get home.

For more ideas on what to do in Southern California, find the Visitor's Information Centers at the Arco Towers in downtown L.A., and at Horton Plaza in downtown San Diego. Ask about special programs for kids at all the parks and museums you visit—almost all have them. Look for colorful guides and brochures at many museums and restaurants. A good way to find out about special events for kids is to look at the local papers' "Events" sections on Thursdays and Fridays. They have special lists of things for kids to do.

ENJOY!

T·R·A·V·E·L D·I·A·R·Y

When I get home, the first thing I will tell my friends is ———
——————————————————.

If I have to write about my trip for school, I will tell my ——————.

teacher about ———————————

The best day of the trip was ————— because ————

——————————————————.

My favorite souvenir is ———————————

I got it at ———————————. I have everything I

collected on this trip in my ————————————

The next trip I take, I want to go to ——————— with

——————. If I come back to Southern California,

——————————————————.

I will go to ———————

❖ ❖ ❖

C·A·L·E·N·D·A·R

JANUARY

Tournament of Roses Parade, Pasadena/
New Year's Parade (818) 449-4100
Beverly Hills Dog Show, LA
Mummer's Day Parade, Balboa Park, SD
New Year's Day Handicap (sailboat
regatta), SD Bay
Penguin Day Ski Fest (water skiing), SD
World Frisbee® Tournament, LA

FEBRUARY

Chinese New Year, LA (213) 617-0396
Mexican Mardi Gras, Olvera Street, LA
Pacific Indoor Rodeo, SD
Spirit of the Whales Festival, Dana Point
(714) 496-2274
Laguna Beach Winter Carnival, Laguna
Beach (714) 494-1018

MARCH

Festival of the Swallows, San Juan
Capistrano (714) 493-4700
Ocean Beach Kite Festival, SD (619)
223-1175
San Diego Crew Classic, Mission Bay, SD
(619) 222-0336
Girl's Day in Little Tokyo, LA (213)
626-3067
Blessing of the Animals, Olvera Street, LA
(213) 625-5045

JULY

Ringling Brothers Circus, Forum, LA
Summer Puppet Theater, Balboa Park, SD
Laguna Beach Living Art Pageant, Laguna
Beach (714) 494-1147
Surf, Sand, and Sandcastle Days, Imperial
Beach (619) 423-8300
Jr. World Golf Championships, Torrey
Pines, SD (619) 453-8148
Del Mar Thoroughbred Club Racing,
Del Mar

AUGUST

Character Boat Parade, Newport Beach
(714) 644-8211
International Surf Festival, Hermosa Beach
America's Finest City Week, SD (619)
232-3101
World Body Surfing Championships,
Oceanside
Miramar Air Show, SD (619) 537-1011
Ocean Beach Sand Sculpture
Championship, SD
Little Tokyo Nisei Festival, LA (213)
626-3067
Santa Monica Sports and Art Festival, LA
(213) 458-8311

SEPTEMBER

Los Angeles County Fair, Pomona (714)
623-3111
Mexican Independence Day, Olvera Street,
LA (213) 625-5045
Cabrillo Festival, Point Loma, SD (619)
232-3101
LA Street Scene, LA (213) 626-0428
Los Angeles Birthday, LA
Thunderboat Regatta, SD

To obtain information about events for which no phone numbers are listed,
call the local Chamber of Commerce:
Los Angeles: (213) 629-0711
San Diego: (619) 232-0124
Balboa Park: (619) 239-9628

APRIL

Renaissance Pleasure Faire, Paramount Ranch, LA (818) 889-3150
Lakeside Western Days and Rodeo, SD County

MAY

Cinco de Mayo, LA & SD (213) 625-5025; (619) 232-0124
Fiesta de la Primavera, Old Town, SD (619) 232-3101
National Horse Show, Del Mar
Boy's Day in Little Tokyo, LA (213) 626-3067

JUNE

Corpus Christi Festival, Mt. Palomar, SD County
Southern California Exposition, Del Mar (619) 232-3101
National Shakespeare Festival, SD (619) 239-2255

OCTOBER

Sandcastle Tournament, Newport Beach
Festival of Masks, Hancock Park, LA
San Diego Zoo Birthday, Balboa Park, SD (619) 234-3153
Haunted Museum, Balboa Park, SD

NOVEMBER

Hollywood Christmas Parade, LA (213) 469-8311
Mother Goose Parade, El Cajon, SD County (619) 232-3101
Doo-Dah Parade, Pasadena (213) 795-9311
Baja 1000 KM, Baja CA Peninsula

DECEMBER

Boat Parade, Newport Beach
Las Posadas, Old Town, SD
Las Posadas, Olvera Street, LA (213) 625-5045
Parade of Lights, Mission and SD bays, SD (619) 232-3101
Long Beach Christmas Water Parade, LA (213) 436-3645

A·P·P·E·N·D·I·X

Admission prices and times are continually changing. To be sure of current rates and hours of operation, call ahead.

BALBOA PARK INFORMATION CENTER (619) 239-0512. 1549 El Prado, San Diego. 9:30 A.M.–4:30 P.M., daily.

Aerospace Museum/International Aerospace Hall of Fame (619) 234-8291. 10:00 A.M.–4:30 P.M., daily. $3.50/adult; $1.00/17 & under child.

Centro Cultural de La Raza (619) 235-6135. Noon–5:00 P.M., Wed.–Sun. Free.

Natural History Museum (619) 232-3821. 10:00 A.M.–4:30 P.M., daily. $3.00/adult; $1.00/6–18 child; free/under 6 & military.

Old Globe Theatre (619) 239-2255. Evening performances most of the year, Tues.–Sun.; weekend matinees. Prices vary according to performance. Call for information.

Reuben H. Fleet Space Theater and Science Center (619) 238-1168. 9:30 A.M.–9:30 P.M., Sun.-Thurs.; 9:30 A.M.–10:30 P.M., Fri. & Sat. Call for show times and admission prices.

San Diego Hall of Champions (619) 234-2544. 10:00 A.M.–4:30 P.M., Mon.–Sat.; noon–5:00 P.M., Sun. $2.00/adult; $1.00/senior citizen, student, & military; $.50/6–17 child; free/under 6.

San Diego Model Railroad Museum (619) 696-0199. 11:00 A.M.–4:00 P.M., Fri.; 11:00 A.M.–5:00 P.M., Sat. & Sun. $1.00/adult; free/child, Fri. Donations accepted Sat. & Sun.

San Diego Museum of Art (619) 232-7931. 10:00 A.M.–4:30 P.M., Tues.–Sun. $4.00/adult; $3.00/senior citizen & military; $2.00/13–18 child; $1.00/6–12 child; free/under 6.

San Diego Museum of Man (619) 239-2001. 10:00 A.M.–4:30 P.M., daily. $2.00/adult; $.25/6–16 child; free/under 6. Free first Tuesday of the month.

Timken Art Gallery (619) 239-5548. 10:00 A.M.–4:30 P.M., Tues.–Sat.; 1:30 P.M.–4:30 P.M., Sun. Free.

CABRILLO NATIONAL MONUMENT (619) 293-5450. End of Cabrillo Memorial Dr., Point Loma, San Diego. 9:00 A.M.–7:25 P.M., daily. $1.00/person or $3.00/car.

DISNEYLAND (714) 999-4565. 1313 Harbor Blvd., Anaheim. Open daily; call for specific hours, which change according to season. $21.50/adult; $17.25/senior citizen; $16.50/3–11 child; free/under 3.

EL PUEBLO DE LOS ANGELES (213) 628-1274. Olvera St. across from Union Depot, Los Angeles. 10:00 A.M.–3:00 P.M., Mon.–Fri.; 10:00 A.M.–4:00 P.M., Sat. Free.

EXPOSITION PARK   (213) 749-5884. 3990 S. Menlo Ave., Los Angeles. 9:00 A.M.–9:00 P.M., daily.

Aerospace Museum   (213) 744-2080. 10:00 A.M.–5:00 P.M., daily. Free.

Afro-American Museum   (213) 744-7432. 10:00 A.M.–5:00 P.M., daily. Free.

California Museum of Science & Industry
(213) 744-7400. 10:00 A.M.–5:00 P.M., daily. Free.

Coliseum   (213) 747-7111. 8:30 A.M.–4:30 P.M., Mon.–Fri. $1.00/person.

Los Angeles Museum of Natural History
(213) 744-3414. 10:00 A.M.–5:00 P.M., Tues.–Sun. $3.00/adult; $1.50/student & senior citizen; $.75/5–12 child; free/under 5.

Mitsubishi Imax Theater   (213) 744-2014/2015. 10:00 A.M.–9:00 P.M., daily. $4.75/adult, one show ($7.00, two shows; $8.50, three shows); $3.50/senior citizen; $3.00/3–17 child & student with I.D. Admission to the 9:00 P.M. show, *Chronos*, is $5.00 for everyone. Special group rates are available for groups of twenty or more.

Swimming Stadium   (213) 748-8479. 2:30 P.M.–5:00 P.M., Mon.–Fri.; 1:00 P.M.–5:00 P.M., Sat. & Sun. $1.00/adult; $.50/17 & under.

FARMERS MARKET   (213) 933-9211. W. Third and Fairfax, Los Angeles. Winter: 9:00 A.M.–6:30 P.M., Mon.–Sat.; 10:00 A.M.–5:00 P.M., Sun. Summer: 9:00 A.M.–7:00 P.M., Mon.– Sat.; 10:00 A.M.–5:00 P.M., Sun. Free.

GRAND CENTRAL MARKET   (213) 624-2378. 315 S. Broadway (between Third and Fourth), Los Angeles. 9:00 A.M.–6:00 P.M., Mon.–Sat.; 10:00 A.M.–4:00 P.M., Sun. Free.

HOLLYWOOD WAX MUSEUM   (213) 462-8860. 6767 Hollywood Blvd., Hollywood. 10:00 A.M.–midnight, Sun.–Thurs.; 10:00 A.M.–2:00 A.M., Fri. & Sat. $6.00/adult; $5.00/13–17 child, senior citizen & military; $4.00/6–12 child; free/under 6.

KNOTT'S BERRY FARM   (714) 220-5200. 8039 Beach Blvd., Buena Park. Open daily; call for specific hours, which change according to season. $16.95/adult; $12.95/3–11 child & senior citizen; free/under 3.

LA BREA TAR PITS/GEORGE C. PAGE MUSEUM
(213) 936-2230. 5801 Wilshire Blvd., Hancock Park, Los Angeles. 10:00 A.M.–5:00 P.M.,Tues.–Sun. $3.00/adult; $1.50/student & senior citizen; $.75/5–18 child; free/under 5. Free second Tuesday of every month.

L.A. CHILDREN'S MUSEUM   (213) 687-8800. 310 N. Main St., Los Angeles. Open daily; call for specific hours, which change according to season. $4.00/adult & child; free/under 2.

L.A. COUNTY MUSEUM OF ART   (213) 857-6010. 5905 Wilshire Blvd., Los Angeles. 10:00 A.M.–5:00 P.M., Tues.–Fri.; 10:00 A.M.–6:00 P.M., Sat. & Sun. $3.00/adult, $1.50/senior citizen & student; $.75/child.

L.A. ZOO   (213) 666-4090. 5333 Zoo Dr., Los Angeles. 10:00 A.M.–5:00 P.M., daily, winter; 10:00 A.M.–6:00 P.M., daily, summer. $4.50/adult; $3.50/senior citizen; $2.00/2–12 child; free/under 2.

MAGIC MOUNTAIN   (805) 255-4100. Magic Mountain Pkwy., Valencia. 10:00 A.M.–10:00 P.M., Sun.–Thurs.; 10:00 A.M.–midnight, Fri. & Sat. in summer. Call for winter hours. $18.00/over 48″; $9.00/under 48″ & senior citizen; free/under 2. Parking, $3.00.

MEDIEVAL TIMES CASTLE   (714) 521-4740. 7662 Beach Blvd., Buena Park. Call for show times. $26.00–28.00/adult; $18.00/under 12.

MISSION DE SAN JUAN CAPISTRANO   (714) 493-1111. Camino Capistrano, San Juan Capistrano. 7:30 A.M.–5:00 P.M., daily. $2.00/adult; $1.00/11 & under.

NBC TELEVISION STUDIO TOUR   (818) 840-3537. 3000 W. Alameda St., Burbank. 8:30 A.M.–4:00 P.M., Mon.–Fri.; 10:00 A.M.–4:00 P.M., Sat.; 10:00 A.M.–2:00 P.M., Sun. $6.00/adult; $4.00/5–14 child; free/under 5. Special children's tours are given in May and November. Call for details.

OLD TOWN STATE PARK   (619) 237-6770. 2645 San Diego Ave., San Diego. Daily. Free.

PORTS O'CALL VILLAGE/WHALER'S WHARF   (213) 831-0287. Berth 77, San Pedro. 11:00 A.M.–9:00 P.M., daily. Free.

RAGING WATERS   (714) 592-6453. Via Verde, San Dimas. Open June–Oct. Call for hours. $12.95/adult, $8.95/4–11 child; free/under 4.

SAN DIEGO CHILDREN'S MUSEUM   (619) 450-0767.
8657 Villa La Jolla Dr., La Jolla. Noon–5:00 P.M., Wed.–Fri.;
10:00 A.M.–5:00 P.M., Sat.; noon–5:00 P.M., Sun.; noon–
5:00 P.M., Tues., groups only. $2.75/adult & child; $1.25/
senior citizen; free/under 2.

SAN DIEGO MARITIME MUSEUM   (619) 234-9153.
1306 N. Harbor Dr., San Diego. 9:00 A.M.–8:00 P.M., daily.
$4.00/adult; $3.00/16–18 junior; $1.00/child.

SAN DIEGO ZOO   (619) 234-3153. Balboa Park, San
Diego. 9:00 A.M.–4:00 P.M., daily, Labor Day–June; 9:00 A.M.–
6:00 P.M., daily, July–Labor Day. General admission: $8.50/
adult; $2.50/3–15 child; free/under 3. Deluxe package
(includes guided bus tour, Skyfari, Children's Zoo):
$13.00/adult; $6.00/3–15 child; free/under 3.

SCRIPPS AQUARIUM   (619) 534-4086. 8602 La Jolla
Shores Dr., La Jolla. 9:00 A.M.–5:00 P.M., daily. Free.

SEAPORT VILLAGE   (619) 235-4013. 849 W. Harbor Dr.,
San Diego. 10:00 A.M.–9:00 P.M., daily. Free.

SEA WORLD   (619) 226-3901. 1720 South Shores Rd., San
Diego. 9:00 A.M.–dusk, daily. Ticket office closes 1½ hours
earlier. $17.95/adult; $11.95/3–11 child & senior citizen;
free/under 3. Call for special holiday and summer evening
hours. Parking, free.

SPRUCE GOOSE/QUEEN MARY,   (213) 435-3511. Pier J,
Long Beach Harbor. 10:00 A.M.–6:00 P.M., daily, winter (box
office closes at 4:00 P.M.); 9:00 A.M.–9:00 P.M., daily, summer
(box office closes at 8:00 P.M.). $14.50/adult; $8.50/6–12
child; free/under 6. Admission good for both attractions.
Parking, $1.00.

UNIVERSAL STUDIOS   (818) 508-9600. Universal City.
8:00 A.M.–4:00 P.M., daily. $16.95/adult; $11.95/3–11 child;
$11.50/senior citizen; free/under 3. Parking, $2.00.

WILD ANIMAL PARK, SAN DIEGO   (619) 234-6541.
15500 San Pasqual Rd., Escondido. 9:00 A.M.–5:00 P.M., daily,
mid-March–mid-June; 9:00 A.M.–4:00 P.M., daily, Nov.–Feb.;
9:00 A.M.–6:00 P.M., daily, mid-June–Labor Day. $12.95/adult;
$6.20/3–15 child; free/under 3. Ticket package includes
entrance, monorail, all shows, and exhibits. Parking, $1.00.

WILL ROGERS PARK & MUSEUM   (213) 454-8212.
14253 Sunset Blvd., Pacific Palisades. 8:00 A.M.–6:00 P.M.,
daily, park; 10:00 A.M.–5:00 P.M., daily, museum. $3.00/car;
$10.00/van; $20.00/bus.

C·A·R G·A·M·E·S

Long car rides don't have to be boring or drive you crazy. Playing games will make the time fly. You don't have to sit still and get sore, stiff, and restless either. Stretch out and move your tired muscles with some easy car exercises. They'll keep you from wishing you could roll down the window and scream or kick open the door and jump out.

Games are for fun, so laugh it up and play the ride away.

Things to take along on any long ride: something hard and flat to write on—like a tray, board, or large hardcover book

> coloring pens, pencils, or crayons
> pad of paper or notebook
> deck of cards
> books to read

WORD GAMES:

Think of as many names as you can for each letter of the alphabet.
D: Debbie, Doug, Diane, Denise, Dan, and so on.

Look for each letter of the alphabet on car license plates as they pass (you can skip the hard-to-find letters Q and Z).

Make words out of the letters you see on car license plates.
For example, for 125 BHV, say "beehive."

Packing for your trip: Name things you can put in your suitcase starting with the letter A, then B, then C, and so on.
For example: Apple, Baseball, Cat, Dictionary (they don't really *have* to be things you need on your trip).

COUNTING GAMES:

Watch car license plates and count the numbers, starting with zero. See who can reach 9 first. Or keep counting to 20; it takes longer.

Find the most: Pick something to count and see who can find the most. You can pick things like green cars, stop signs, license plates from California, people driving with hats on, kids in cars, and so on.

GUESSING GAMES:

20 Questions: Think of something for the others to guess. They ask you questions to try to figure out what it is. You can only answer "yes" or "no." If no one guesses in twenty questions, you win. Or you can just let them keep asking questions until someone figures it out.

Pictionary (like dictionary, but with pictures): Like 20 Questions, someone is "it" and thinks of something that everyone else tries to guess. You draw pictures to give them clues and hints—but you can't draw what the answer is. You could pick the name of your school. Then, for clues, you could draw your classroom, desk, schoolbook, lunch box, or teacher—or anything else you might think of. Draw pictures until someone guesses what it is you're thinking of.

DRAWING:

One person draws a mark, line, shape, letter, or number, and someone else has to make a picture out of it.

STORIES:

One person starts to make up a story. The next person has to add the next line or sentence to the story; then on to the next person. Everyone in the car takes a turn making up the story line by line. It can turn out to be a pretty funny story. You might even end up on the moon with a _____ .

Make up a travel friend: This is your chance to say anything you want about your trip. You pretend that you have an invisible friend taking the trip with you. Only you can see and hear your friend, so you have to tell everyone else what your friend is saying. Does he or she like your car? Where does she want to go tomorrow? What does he like to eat? You can say ANYTHING. Make up

a story about where your friend is from, what his or her family is like—or whatever you want.

CARDS:

Bring along a deck of cards and play your favorite games. Or, if there's room, you can turn a hat over and try to toss the cards into it. You have to throw them as if they were tiny Frisbees.

MOVEMENT GAMES:

Charade: Someone acts out a kind of animal (or anything else) using only face and hands. Everyone else has to guess what she or he is.

Simon Says: Choose someone to be Simon. Everyone else has to do whatever Simon says— but only when Simon says, "Simon says. . . . " If Simon doesn't say this and you do what he or she says, you goof. Like this: "Simon says, 'Touch your nose with your right hand.' " (Simon touches his nose. Everyone else does, too.) Simon gives lots of directions, then he sneaks in an order without saying "Simon says" but does it anyway. If anyone follows, he or she goofs.

Statue: Everyone playing this game freezes into a statue. See who can stay that way the longest without moving.

Making faces: Someone is "it." He or she makes a face—sad, goofy, happy, sleepy, cranky—and the other person has to imitate the face. This simple game is really a crack-up.

EXERCISES:

You'll be amazed at how much exercise you can get while riding in a car. You can't swim, run, or throw a ball, but you can work out by stretching your muscles. Make up your own stretches, or do the ones below. Remember to hold one stretch to the count of ten before beginning another. And don't forget to take a deep breath and blow it out slowly with every stretch. It's "car yoga."

Touch your toes. Stretch your arms straight out. Spin them in circles. Twist around as far as you can. Reach for the ceiling. Bend your head back. Bend it forward. Press your hands down on the seat next to you and try to lift yourself off the seat. Flex your feet up, then down; point your toes. Repeat this ten times. You'll be surprised at how good this feels for stiff muscles.

Answers to Puzzles

page 8

Here are some; can you think of more?

page 9

DEAR	DARN	ROAR
DEAD	DUNE	READ
DARE	DOER	REAR
DEAN	DONE	RODE
NEAR	UNDO	RARE
NUDE	NONE	RUDE
NERD	NOUN	NEON

	Post office		Helicopter service
	First aid		Car rental
	Restaurant		Nursery
	Train service		Bathroom
	For the disabled		Telephones

127

page 10

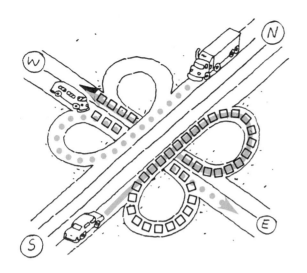

page 16

San Diego	*sahn dee-AY-go*
Catalina	*kah-tah-LEE-nah*
San Nicholas	*sahn NEEK-oh-lahs*
La Brea	*lah BRAY-ah*
Mojave	*mo-HAHV-ee*

page 17

Alcala	*ahl-CAHL-ah*
Capistrano	*kah-pee-STRAHN-oh*
San Juan	*sahn wahn*
Junipero Serra	*hoon-ee-PAY-roh SAYR-rah*

page 18

presidios	*pray-SEE-dyos*
nuestra	*new-AYS-trah*
reina	*ray-EEN-ah*

page 18

CABRIL**L**O	He discovered San Diego Bay.
MIS**S**ION	San Juan Capistrano is one.
SAN DI**E**GO	The first mission was built here.
RANC**H**O	First established by land grant in 1775.
FOR**T**	Built to protect early missions.
SMIT**H**	"Knight in Buckskin"
PRESIDI**O**	Towns built around forts.
F**U**R	Skins sought by trappers.
SANTO	Spanish word for "saint."
S**E**RRA	Franciscan friar.

page 20

Cabrillo	Point Loma
California	Balboa Park
Los Angeles	Native Americans
Franciscans	San Diego

page 23

1-b; 2-a; 3-b; 4-c; 5-a; 6-c; 7-a; 8-a; 9-b

page 24

serape	*say-RAH-pay*
Tijuana	*tee-WAHN-nah*

page 30

guacamole	*gwa-ka-MOE-lay*
tortilla	*tore-TEE-ya*

page 34

burrito	Mexico
wonton	China
baklava	Greece
lasagna	Italy
sushi	Japan
dumpling	England
curry	India

page 39

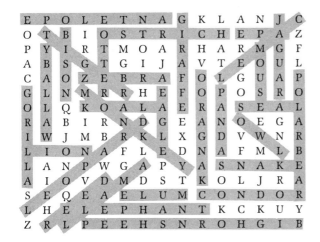

page 47

equestrian and yachting

page 50

MUSEUM	DINOSAURS
ADOBE	MINIBUS
FOSSIL	CAPSULES
ROCKETS	COMPUTER

page 53

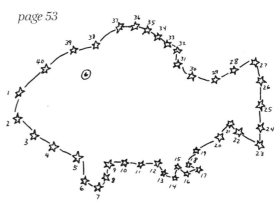

page 61

SNOW WHITE
BAMBI
PLUTO
WINNIE THE POOH
PETER PAN
MICKEY MOUSE
DONALD DUCK
DUMBO
MAD HATTER
CINDERELLA
BASHFUL
TIGGER
GOOFY
MINNIE MOUSE

page 65

1. BUENA Park, California
2. Walter and CORDELIA Knott
3. YULETIDE Fantasy on Parade
4. GHOST Town
5. DENVER–Rio Grande train
6. Calico SALOON
7. BUFFALO Nickel Arcade
8. Red Cliff ENGINE Number 41
9. Montezuma's REVENGE
10. Toyota Good Time THEATRE
11. Camp SNOOPY

page 70

page 85

page 80

7	dingo	10	giraffe
5	condor	4	black bear
8	elephant	21	tiger
11	gorilla	15	otter
12	hedgehog	1	alligator
18	pelican	14	kangaroo
9	fox	2	anteater
16	owl	22	zebra
3	bison	20	spider monkey
17	panda	19	platypus
13	jaguar	6	coyote

page 88

page 91

antique bison ⟶ BUFFALO
sabertooth cat ⟶ MOUNTAIN LION
dire wolf ⟶ WOLF
merriam teraform (bird) ⟶ CONDOR/VULTURE
short-faced bear ⟶ BLACK BEAR

page 95

cloud chamber — Reuben H. Fleet Space Theater and Science Center

dinosaur skeleton — Natural History Museum

sculpture — San Diego Museum of Art

Padre uniform — Hall of Champions

arrowhead — Museum of Man

piñata — Centro Cultural de la Raza

hot-air balloon — Aerospace Museum

page 100

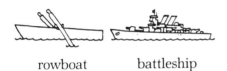

rowboat   battleship

paddleboat   ocean liner   sailboat

page 103

I swam south with the whales. See ya!

page 110

page 112

```
F  L  T  R  Z  A  O  L  R  D  S  T
R  G  O  L  D  D  U  S  T  M  A  L
I  N  T  D  R  G  G  F  Z  R  O  O
Z  I  D  G  B  N  U  G  G  E  T  R
G  O  L  R  U  Z  T  I  A  U  T  P
I  O  D  N  L  Y  F  A  B  Q  U  R
S  D  T  S  L  I  A  R  A  T  L  D
Y  R  A  N  I  U  G  G  R  S  T  U
R  I  N  G  O  T  S  I  L  V  B  O
N  R  E  I  N  G  F  O  I  A  G  T
```

PHOTO CREDITS
■■■■■■■■■■■■■■■■

Pages	Courtesy of
7	State of California, Dept. of Conservation, Division of Mines & Geology; Photo by Thomas Dibblee, Jr.
13	San Diego Convention & Visitors Bureau
17	San Diego Historical Society—Ticor Collection
26	Greater Los Angeles Visitors and Convention Bureau
27	Seaport Village
29	Greater Los Angeles Visitors and Convention Bureau
29	Waterfront Promotions; Photo by C. R. Learn
30	Bazaar del Mundo
32	Medieval Times
38	Los Angeles Zoo
44–45	Greater Los Angeles Visitors and Convention Bureau
52	Griffith Observatory, Dr. E. C. Krupp

Pages	Courtesy of
54	Greater Los Angeles Visitors and Convention Bureau
57	Greater Los Angeles Visitors and Convention Bureau
58	Wrather Port Properties, Ltd.
60	© The Walt Disney Company
63–64	Knott's Berry Farm
66	Knott's Berry Farm
67	Six Flags Magic Mountain
68	Raging Waters
71	Universal Studios
74–75	U.S. Dept. of Interior, National Park Service; Photo by Richard Frear
81	San Diego Convention & Visitors Bureau
82	© Zoological Society of San Diego
84	Sea World
86–87	Sea World
91	San Diego Convention & Visitors Bureau

Pages	Courtesy of
95	San Diego Museum of Man/Laura Walcher Public Relations
96	San Diego Union-Tribune Publishing Company; Photo by Jim Baird
98	San Diego Convention & Visitors Bureau
98	Maritime Museum Association of San Diego
101	California Department of Transportation
102	San Diego Historical Society—Ticor Collection
106	San Diego Convention & Visitors Bureau
112	San Diego Historical Society—Ticor Collection

I·N·D·E·X

Aerospace Building Two, 48
Aerospace Museum and
  International Aerospace Hall of
  Fame, 9, 96
Aerospace Museum One, 48
Afro-American Museum, 51
Air and Space Garden, 48
American Indians. *See* Native
  Americans
Amusement Parks, 13, 24, 57,
  59–69
Anza Borrego Desert State Park,
  73–74
Aquariums, 84–89
Avila Adobe, 42

Baja California, 16
Balboa Park, 14, 79, 80, 90–93
Barnsdall Park, 56
Beaches, 5–6, 13
  in L.A., 56–57
  in San Diego, 76, 101, 104, 106–8
Berkeley, 99
Beverly Hills, 24, 55
Bicycling, 57, 73, 97, 105

Broadway Pier, 98, 99
Buena Park, 63

Cabrillo, Juan, 15–16, 103
Cabrillo National Monument, 103–4
Cabrillo Point, 103–4
California Museum of Science and
  Industry, 48–49
Centro Cultural de la Raza, 96
Chicano Park, 101
Children's Museum of San Diego,
  108
Chinatown, 26, 40, 43
City Hall, 40
Climate, 5, 12
Coronado Bridge, 99, 101
Coronado Island, 16, 99, 101–2,
  103, 104
Coronado Islands, 7, 103, 104
Cultural Center, Tijuana, 113
Cuyamaca State Park, 110

Death Valley, 75
Disney, Walt, 23, 59
Disneyland, 35, 59–62

Elysian Park, 56
Embarcadero, 98
Exposition Park, 47–51

Farmer's Market, 26
Freeways, 8–10, 40, 76

Geology, 7
Grand Central Public Market, 26
Griffith Park, 38, 51–52

Hall of Champions, 93
Hancock Park, 44, 45
Heritage Park, 105
Hiking, 52, 57, 74, 75, 108, 109,
  110–11
Historical Society, 42
History of Southern California,
  14–23
Hollywood, 22–23, 29, 53–55
Hollywood Wax Museum, 55
Horton Plaza, 28, 114
Hotel del Coronado, 101–2

Idyllwild, 75

Joshua Tree National Monument, 74
Julian, 21, 112
Julian Museum, 112

Knott's Berry Farm, 63–66

La Brea Tar Pits, 44–45
L.A. Children's Museum, 34, 43–44
L.A. County Fair, 20
L.A. County Museum of Art, 45
Laguna Mountain Recreation Area, 111
La Jolla, 6, 89, 107–8
La Jolla Cove, 107–8
La Jolla Shores Beach, 107
L.A. Zoo, 13, 38–39
Lighthouse, Cabrillo Point, 16, 103–4
Little Tokyo, 26, 40, 42
Lindbergh Field, 9
Long Beach, 13, 58
Los Angeles, 35
    attractions, 6, 38–39, 40, 42–45, 47–72
    history, 18–19, 22–23
    restaurants, 29–30, 32, 34, 58
    shopping, 24–26
Los Angeles Harbor, 26
Los Angeles International Airport (LAX), 9
Los Angeles Museum of Natural History, 50–51

Magic Mountain, 66–68
Mann's Chinese Theater, 54
Medea, 99
Medieval Times Castle, 32
Mexico, 7, 11, 24, 30, 113
Mission Bay, 29, 82, 105
Mission Bay Park, 105
Mission Beach, 106
Mission de San Juan Capistrano, 17
Missions, 16–18, 105

Mitsubishi Imax Theater, 47–48
Model Railroad Museum, 94
Morongo Indian Reservation, 74
Movies, 53–55, 71–72
    history of, 22–23, 53–54
    theaters, 47–48, 52, 54, 55, 56, 61–62, 65, 72, 91–92
Mukiteo Lighthouse, 27
Museums, 13, 24, 110, 112, 113
    in Los Angeles, 43–45, 47–52, 55
    in San Diego, 9, 15, 90–96, 98–99, 103, 105, 108
Museum of Man, 15, 95

Natural History Museum, 91
Native Americans, 14–16, 74, 95, 96, 110
Nautical museums, 98–99
NBC Studio Tour, 70–71

Old Globe Theater, 94
Old Plaza, 19, 42
Old Plaza Fire Station, 42
Old Town, 18, 104–5
Olvera Street, 26, 40, 42
Olympics, 47, 48, 51

Pacific Beach, 106
Pacific Ocean, 5–6, 9
Page Museum, 44–45
Palisades Park, 57
Palm Springs, 74
Palos Verdes Hills, 6
Places of Learning, 88
Playgrounds, 56, 87, 97
Plaza Rio Tijuana, 113
Point Loma, 7, 16, 102, 104
Pomona, 20
Ports O' Call, 26
Presidio Park, 18, 105
Pueblo de Los Angeles, 40, 42

Queen Mary, 13, 58

Raging Waters, 68–69
Restaurants, 29–34, 62, 64, 68, 69, 104
Reuben H. Fleet Space Theater and Science Center, 91–2
Rodeo Drive, 24, 55
Roxbury Park, 56

San Andreas Fault, 7
San Diego, 76
    attractions, 9, 11, 79–99, 101–8
    history, 14–18, 21
    restaurants, 29, 104
    shopping, 27–28, 88, 104
San Diego Bay, 27, 29, 98
San Diego de Alcala, 16–17
San Diego Harbor, 15
San Diego Museum of Art, 94
San Diego Wild Animal Park, 82–84
San Diego Zoo, 13, 79–82
San Jacinto Mountains, 74, 75
Santa Catalina Island, 7, 73
Santa Monica, 56–57
Santa Monica Beach, 56–57
Santa Monica Pier, 57
Scripps Aquarium and Museum, 89
Seaport Village, 27
Sea World, 84, 86–89
Serra, Father Junipero, 16–17, 105
Serra Museum, 105
Shelter Island, 102
Smith, Jedidiah, 21
Spanish exploration, 14, 15–19
Sports, 47, 56, 93
Spruce Goose, 13, 58
Star of India, 99

Tail of the Pup, 29
Theater, 58, 68, 94–95
Tijuana, 113
Timken Art Gallery, 94
Torrey Pines State Reserve, 109

Union Station, 40
Universal Studios, 71–72
University of California, Los Angeles
   (UCLA), 56
University of Southern California, 47

Visitor's Information Center, 40, 114

Walk of Fame, 54
Water sports, 12, 51, 57, 68–69, 73,
   102, 103, 105–8
Westwood, 56

Wilcox, Horace, 22
Will Rogers Museum, 56
Will Rogers Park, 56

Zoos, 13, 24, 38–39, 52, 67,
   79–84